Mad About Movies #9

Mad About Movies #9

Editors
Gary J. Svehla
Aurelia Susan Svehla

Graphic Design Interior
Gary J. Svehla

Front Cover
Aurelia Susan Svehla

Copy Editor
Janet Atkinson

Writers
Nicholas Anez
Arthur Joseph Lundquist
Gary J. Svehla
Steve Vertlieb

Special Thanks
Warner Home Video; Fox Home Video; Raro Video; Universal Home Video; Scream! Factory; Kino Home Video; Matt Berry; Scott Essman; Susan Svehla

Publisher
Midnight Marquee Press, Inc.

Mad About Movies #9, November 2014, is copyright © 2014 by Gary J. Svehla; *Mad About Movies* is published annually at 9721 Britinay Lane, Parkville, MD 21234; e-mail Gary Svehla at midmargary@aol.com; websites: http://www.midmar.com; phone: 410-665-1198

Regular issues of the magazine are available for $10 (plus $1 shipping Media Mail; $7 Priority Mail) and may be ordered only one issue in advance. We ship internationally, but please request current international shipping rates before placing your order.

Articles and art should be transmitted electronically (or via snail mail) and will remain the property of the writer/artist or copyright holder, who will retain all rights. If material intended for publication is sent to us via regular mail, it is the sender's responsibility to include return postage. No responsibility is taken for unsolicited material.

Editorial views expressed by writers are not necessarily those of the publisher, Midnight Marquee Press. Nothing may be reproduced or shared in any media without the expressed written permission of the publisher. Letters of comment addressed to *Midnight Marquee* or Gary Svehla and/or Susan Svehla will be considered for publication, unless the writer requests otherwise.

We enthusiastically solicit articles and artwork from professionals and novices alike, but it is best to discuss potential submissions in advance. Remember, *Mad About Movies* emphasizes the classics of the Golden Age of cinema including film noir, mystery, thrillers, Westerns, comedies, suspense, etc.

Mad About Movies Contents

3 Always ... Mad About Movies (Editorial)
by Gary J. Svehla

4 Tarzan, Lord of RKO
by Arthur Joseph Lundquist

14 *The Whistler*: Mystery, Shadows and Suspense On The Cheap
by Gary J. Svehla

40 Fred MacMurray: Hollywood's Invisible Legend
by Nicholas Anez

50 Get Your Kicks on *Route 66*
by Steve Vertlieb

58 *Thriller*: Season One's Best in Crime and Suspense
by Gary J. Svehla

69 A Comparison of *One Sunday Afternoon* and *The Strawberry Blonde*
by Arthur Joseph Lundquist

73 *Mad About Movies* Book Review
by Gary J. Svehla

79 *Mad About Movies* Home Video Review
by Gary J. Svehla

ALWAYS ... MAD ABOUT MOVIES

Editorial Ramblings by Gary J. Svehla

Welcome to issue #9 of *Mad About Movies*, our first issue returning to a larger-format black-and-white interior. Not that we did not love the all-color format, but being able to only produce 40 pages per issue limited our aspirations and ability to get articles into circulation in a more timely manner. Many people missed the use of glossy photos, balanced out with posters and lobby cards. In the former all-color format, we were pretty much limited to using colorful posters and lobby cards, since photos were typically monochrome. Now we can again expand our page count to 100 pages, add some bulk and feature more articles each issue.

But even bigger changes are occurring in the world of home video. Even though this might take years to occur, it appears that the era of the physical silver disc is coming to an end faster than suspected. DVD lasted for the past few decades and Blu-ray lately has become a viable force in the market place as well. But sales of physical media have decreased as online movie viewing and streaming video content has been increasing. Everyone has friends who pay $8 per month for Netflix (subscription rates soon to increase), since the majority of people now stream movie content. With services such as Netflix, Vudu, Comcast Xfinity, Verizon FIOS and others, it is now possible to own streaming content and replay movies as often as the buyer desires (but the movies will only be available as long as the hosting company survives). We have Apple TV, Amazon Fire TV and Ruku and sales of such streaming TV boxes continue to mushroom.

Now the collector, the hobbyist, of course is up in arms over owning movies that exist only in the Cloud. It may be great to own *Wizard of Oz* and to be able to show it as often as possible, but the fact is that the buyer can no longer hold the package in his or her hands, read the liner notes and enclosed graphics, especially those little fact-filled booklets that are very collectible. And with special box sets, collectors get the added bonus of mini-lobby cards or photographs and other little trinkets that make owning the movie extra special. Often the packaging of the movie, with its front and back cover graphics and poster art, alone is worth the total cost—forget about *watching* the movie. And when stacked on a DVD/Blu-ray shelf, a collector can display his collection and proudly show it off to friends, relatives and other collectors. Not so when we own movies in the Cloud. A long list of titles on a TV screen is not quite as impressive.

The writing can be seen on the wall when even companies such as The Warner Archive Collection offers many of their movies at unlimited streaming for $10 per month (including an HD copy of *Curse of the Cat People*). Of course many older collectors (and some not even old) do not own or use computers for entertainment and refuse to stream movies to watch them. Many families do not have Wi-Fi in their homes, so streaming becomes impossible. Therefore, physical media will remain as a niche market for most likely another decade or perhaps two. Most likely fewer titles will be released in the upcoming decade as disc media, and since fewer copies will be pressed and purchased, the cost for owning physical media will most likely increase radically in price (since owning a physical disc to watch movies will become more and more of a specialty product).

Just as national newspapers and magazines are gradually transitioning to digital online incantations of what formerly were print newspapers and magazines, our movies will also be gradually transformed from disc to digital. And unfortunately for some, this will be occurring much faster than many suspected.

But for collectors, books and magazines will most likely survive as hard print copies for quite some time, even though collectors may have to pay through the nose for such niche treasures. As the younger generation rises up, they will more easily accept the concept of digital books, magazines, newspapers and movies as the technological dinosaurs of the past fight to hold their treasured collectables in their hands and store in their cherished household temples to pop culture.

For movies, it is the technological changes that demand the end of physical disc media. As we worked our way up from VHS to laserdisc to DVD and now to Blu-ray, each movie and the extras included along with the movie take up more and more digital space. As we move into UHD (ultra high definition), so-called 4k-resolution, physical media can no longer hold all the digital information on a single disc. And beyond 4k is the 35mm film comparable 8k, which may or may not be the final high definition resolution needed to wow the human eye. But for uncompressed visual and audio data (providing the highest level of resolution), streaming is the only option that allows home audiences to watch these higher resolution formats. I know, I know, many collectors say they are satisfied with VHS or DVD and they don't need higher resolution. But manufacturers are selling to mainstream audiences, younger audiences, who want the absolute best in audio and visual quality or simply desire to be bleeding edge technophiles. We still have a collector's market of fans that own, buy, sell and trade used 16mm prints. A collector's market of mostly elder fans own, buy, sell and trade network radio programs from the Golden Age of Radio. In other words, a niche and very limited market exists for these collectors, much in the same way as a very limited niche audience will always exist for print media that we can hold in our hand and movie and audio discs that we can physically touch. But such media will be flung to the underbelly of society within the next two decades. A few people still use actual typewriters, but just try to buy typewriters today. They too have become a limited niche market. But how long will advocates continue to refurbish and sell old units?

So many people have chimed in that they bought a copy of *Casablanca* on VHS, then bought it on laserdisc, then DVD and finally Blu-ray (often in multiple releases in DVD and Blu-ray), so now they refuse to buy the same movie in UHD (4k) and later 8k. But soon when we buy movies we will not be plopping a silver platter into a media player. That will go the way of 8-track tapes. As science fiction told us for centuries, the future lies in the clouds. The digital Cloud, that is.

Tarzan, Lord of RKO

by Arthur Joseph Lundquist

The human heart is a strange thing. Why does it want what it wants? Universal produced some of the greatest horror movies of the thirties and forties, and yes, when the Universal Legacy Collection DVDs were released, I did eventually buy them. But what sent me running out the door to spend money was news of the DVD release of Universal's remarkably boring *Inner Sanctum Mysteries* with Lon Chaney, Jr. By the same token, two films from Warner Brothers' Dead End Kids series are actual cinema classics (*Dead End* and *Angels With Dirty Faces*). And yet the only time I ever felt actually compelled to shell out cash to observe the work of Leo Gorcey and Huntz Hall was when I discovered some cheap DVD collections of the completely inferior films they made at Monogram as the East Side Kids. And while I will forever honor Bela Lugosi's iconic turns in *Dracula*, *Murders in the Rue Morgue* and *Son of Frankenstein* at Universal, I somehow more actually itch to own his Poverty Row work like *Voodoo Man*, *Invisible Ghost* and *Return of the Ape Man*.

Why? Is it a morbid curiosity to watch beloved stars as their careers start to slip downhill? Or is it a professional interest in seeing how artists rise to the occasion when times are hard? Or is it simple Boomer nostalgia for childhood afternoons misspent watching B-movies that weren't all that good when our parents were kids?

Case in point.

From 1932's *Tarzan the Ape Man* all the way to *Tarzan Finds A Son* in 1939, MGM treated *Tarzan* movies as their top-level releases, with first-class production values and crews dedicated to doing their best work. With 1934's *Tarzan and His Mate* they created one of the great romantic adventures of all time. In the chemistry between Johnny Weissmuller's Tarzan and Maureen O'Sullivan's Jane, an earthy sensuality bridges London sophistication to savage simplicity, something so appealing that daters, spouses and families on their night out could usually all agree to go see a Tarzan movie. With the addition of Johnny Sheffield as Boy in *Tarzan Finds a Son*, the series became more family-friendly. After 1942's *Tarzan's New York Adventure*, Maureen O'Sullivan left the series, taking with her a huge percentage of the female audience. Rather than budget down for a diminished box-office, MGM's executives chose to give up the franchise.

Fortunately, someone existed out there that was just itching to produce *Tarzan* movies. Born in 1890, Sol Lesser had been in moving pictures since he worked in his father's nickelodeon in 1907. By the time of his death in 1980 he was one of the last living links with the first generation of producers in Hollywood. In both the silent and talkie eras he created and sold off chains of movie theaters, acquiring titles and creating production companies to keep his screens filled with product. He produced films with child stars Jackie Coogan, Baby Peggy and Bobby Breen. He made Westerns (lots). He employed Bela Lugosi in the 1934 serial *The Return of Chandu*. He made an important art film adaptation of Thornton Wilder's *Our Town*. He distributed documentaries, and with *Kon Tiki* (1950), earned an Oscar.

But all along he seemed to have had a hankering to make *Tarzan* movies. In 1934 and 1938, when MGM and Johnny Weissmuller pretty much had dibs on the character, Lesser independently produced *Tarzan the Fearless* and *Tarzan's Revenge* with Buster Crabbe and Glenn Morris, respectively, as the ape man. According to an interesting clipping from *The New York World-Telegraph*, in 1936 Lesser was even trying to hire Lou Gehrig to play Tarzan.

In 1942, Lesser saw his chance and left an executive position with RKO to become the official producer of *Tarzan* movies. And only nine months after MGM premiered *Tarzan's New York Adventure*, RKO had its own Tarzan title on theater marquees.

From its opening shot of the RKO logo with the V-For-Victory Dit-Dit-Dit-DAHHHHH of Beethoven's Fifth Symphony, to its ending of Cheetah doing an imitation of Adolph Hitler, *Tarzan Triumphs* (1943) is an unmistakable artifact of the World War II home front. In fact, this jungle adventure is an honest-to-gosh political allegory. Nazi soldiers parachute into Tarzan's jungle and enslave a local hidden city. Tarzan, standing in for isolationist America, tolerates their presence so long as they don't climb his escarpment (a steep cliff separating two level landscapes) and threaten his family. But when his jungle tree house is overrun by booted thugs, Tarzan seizes a knife and proclaims, "Now, Tarzan make war!" And then, as G.E. Blackford wrote for *The New York Journal-American*, "Mr. Schickelgruber might as well give up."

This is a great premise. Come on, who would not want to see the lord of the jungle team up with local tribesmen to drive off foreign invaders? But that, alas, was not going to happen. Not in 1942,

Top: Tarzan (Johnny Weissmuller) battles the Nazis, sadistically evil and mentally challenged, in the first Sol Lesser-produced RKO Tarzan entry, *Tarzan Triumphs*. Bottom: Cheetah, Tarzan, Zandar (Frances Gifford) and Boy (Johnny Sheffield)

and not at RKO. For one thing, in place of Edgar Rice Burroughs' Wazuri tribe of the novels (or the black cannibals and pygmies of the MGM films), individuals who at the time would have had no trouble drinking from a "whites only" fountain in Birmingham inhabited the jungles of RKO almost exclusively. Perhaps it was an effort by Mr. Lesser to simultaneously avoid charges of both racism *and* race mixing, but *Tarzan Triumphs* presents us with an Africa without any black people at all.

Tarzan's battle with the Nazis, who are alternately sadistically evil and mentally challenged, was ideal Saturday fodder for children of the war years. As the reviewer from *PM New York* reported from his seat at the RKO Palace, "The Palace mob, after sitting noncommittally through Monty Wooley's sophisticated *Life Begins at 8:30* (a drama about alcoholism), cheered Tarzan's uninhibited anti-Nazism to the echo."

Along the way, Tarzan's chimp companion Cheetah provides comic relief—lots of comic relief, a seemingly endless amount of comic relief. In the early MGM *Tarzan*s, Cheetah was presented, not as a full-grown chimp, but as a juvenile member of the tribe of intelligent apes who brought up Tarzan as a baby. By the end of that run, however, those dignified, mythic apes had been tossed into the dustbin of history and in their place stood triumphant Cheetah the chimpanzee, comic relief. Even given the debased standard of the later MGM Tarzans, *Tarzan Triumphs* devotes a remarkable amount of screen time to the clowning of Cheetah, which would seem to grow with every successive RKO entry. The diminutive primate gets so much screen time that *somebody* must have been enjoying it, but it raises the camp level of the series far beyond what anyone should have to bear. As a child I always found these scenes insultingly stupid, though as an adult I am impressed by the expressive performances given by the various Cheetahs used over the course of the series.

Tarzan Triumphs takes a gingerly approach to replacing Maureen O'Sullivan. Jane, we are informed, is in Europe visiting family. But a *Tarzan* movie without a cute girl would be unthinkable. So Tarzan spends a lot of time with Zandra, an attractive young lady from that hidden city, adequately portrayed by Frances Gifford, who the year before had been the title heroine of the Republic serial *Jungle Girl*. The script even finds an excuse to get Zandra into Jane's clothing, allowing posters and lobby cards to give the misleading impression the film actually has a Jane. As scripted, Tarzan's relationship with Zandra is all fatherly innocence, but at moments it becomes a little disturbing to watch a shirtless man approaching middle age hanging out with a sweet young thing while his wife is out of town.

It would be unrealistic to expect a medium-level RKO production to compete with the lavish design and polish of the MGM films. Or to hope that an RKO programmer could include those magical underwater scenes in which gold medal Olympic swimmer Weissmuller glides effortlessly in his own element. Yet even after we lower our expectations, the jungle settings of *Tarzan Triumphs* show a noticeable lack of atmosphere or visual interest and are sometimes backed by painted-sky cycloramas that look surprisingly phony. It is a real comedown from the studio that created the atmospheric Gustav Dore jungles of *King Kong* and *The Most Dangerous Game*. In truth, in spite of a fairly generous budget, something lackluster exists about almost every aspect of *Tarzan Triumphs*. The performances by many of the lesser Nazis are notably half-hearted. Nobody, except perhaps Weissmuller and Sheffield, seems to be trying to do his best work, and the uninspired script and direction even put a crimp on them. Even in the big climactic moment when Tarzan announces "Tarzan make war!" director Wilhelm Thiele's set-up and execution of what is obviously intended to be a major applause line is remarkably uninteresting.

Things are much the same in *Tarzan's Desert Mystery* (1943). In fact, this is probably the single most disappointing *Tarzan* film Weissmuller ever made. Again, great premise. Tarzan and Boy fight Nazi thugs in a lost jungle of giant prehistoric lizards. I mean, hey, Tarzan fighting dinosaurs? It is for premises like

this that the exclamation "Cool!" was invented.

Much of the film takes place in a sandy desert, a refreshing change of scene for the series. Even here Tarzan finds kinship with the local wildlife, in this case a wild horse. It is somehow touching to see Tarzan and Boy bonding with the animal and hear Weissmuller speak lines like, "Horse want freedom just like everyone."

Throughout his career, Weissmuller poked fun at his own acting ability, and few people would champion him as a reader of dialogue. Yet he exuded a very real charisma and, especially when sharing the frame with Maureen O'Sullivan or Johnny Sheffield, brought genuine emotional warmth to his scenes that at times can be unexpectedly moving.

In fact, with this film director William Thiele and screenwriter Edward T. Lowe create some of the most endearing Tarzan-Boy interactions of the series. Boy is a shade smarter than his adoptive Dad but never manages to actually put anything over the old man. They exude real love and affection for each other as they muddle through life, seemingly a little lost without Jane to look after them. A scene exists where Tarzan, Boy and Cheetah cuddle up to sleep together, making the sweetest extended family. In moments like that, Thiele and Lowe work actual movie magic. I imagine the typical movie-going kid leaving the theater in 1943, going home and glancing up at his boring father with a sigh of hopeless envy.

It is comedienne Nancy Kelly's thankless task to be this film's Jane-substitute, or, to put it in WWII home front terms, a "Victory Jane." She plays an American stage magician whom Tarzan and Boy find lost in the desert. With her Vaudeville veteran street smarts and wisecracks, Ms.

Tarzan (Johnny Weissmuller) strikes an intense pose, with Nancy Kelly behind him.

Some of the most endearing Tarzan-Boy interactions of the series occur in *Tarzan's Desert Mystery*. They exude real love and affection for one another.

Kelly brings an entirely different, fun dynamic to the Tarzan-Jane relationship. She is endearing as a reluctant adoptive mother to Boy and has a scene with a giant spider that is one of the highlights of the film. The prop spider is way above average (see *World Without End*) and is spookily photographed in shadow to obscure any design imperfections. Any kid who was ever scared by our eight-legged friends will watch with admiration as she stands her ground, vainly chucking rocks at the damned thing while Boy is trapped in a giant web.

The vast majority of *Tarzan's Desert Mystery* takes place in the desert city of Birherari, another of those African locations inhabited by heavily made-up white people, where Nazi agents are organizing a rebellion against the local sheik. Lacking the fish-out-of-water drama that enhanced *Tarzan's New York Adventure*, it is not a particularly interesting setting for our ape-man hero.

It takes us 50 of the film's 70 minutes for our heroes to finally reach that prehistoric jungle. Then what happens? Uh, nothing much happens, really. Tarzan walks around gazing at back projections of a few lizards. The casual filmgoer will probably not realize that this is footage from *One Million B.C.* (1940), while the more maniacal fan will enjoy seeing Tarzan united with familiar lizard friends and take note that some shots appear to be not just *One Million B.C.* stock footage but actual outtakes from that film. This entry's big problem is that the giant lizards don't really *do* anything. Tarzan briefly struggles with some carnivorous plants, but too much time in this jungle is spent with perfectly conventional elephants and lions. The film does so little with its monsters, which are never referred to in the dialogue, that it makes me wonder if earlier drafts of the script had set this scene in an ordinary jungle and the lizards were added late in production to spice up the undistinguished goings-on.

Having made that observation, I was surprised to read in a 1991 issue of *The Big Reel* by Geoff St. Andrews that the synopsis in *Tarzan's Desert Mystery's* official press book contains no mention of dinosaurs or prehistoric jungle, only of skullduggery by Nazis to take over the local sheikdom. Further, he tells us, *Tarzan's Desert Mystery* had originally been filmed as *Tarzan Against the Sahara*, but it was re-shot on Sol Lesser's orders into the form we know today. St. Andrews speculates that the press book gives the film's original storyline, and that the lizards all came from the re-shoot, perhaps directed by the film's associate producer, Kurt Neumann. Which makes sense, since Kurt Neumann, as we all know, would go on to become the auteur of *Rocketship X-M* (1950), *Kronos* (1957) and *The Fly* (1958), showing a real affinity for pulp sci-fi.

And indeed, the next RKO *Tarzan* entry, *Tarzan and the Amazons* (1945), directed solely by Neumann, is a genuine scientific romance in the Edgar Rice Burroughs mode, with a storyline about a lost civilization where women rule that comes straight out of a pulp magazine.

From its first moments, Neumann shows a better knack for the material than Thiele. His junglescapes are darker and more mysterious, given a three-dimensional feel by Neumann and cinematographer Archie Stout, and he places lots of lush foliage between actors and camera. And while the prior two films had used (and reused) maybe one or two matte paintings, *Amazons* starts out with a lot of matte paintings. Really cool looking matte paintings of huge, impressive mountains and cliffs and stone gorges. The paintings are obviously not real, but hey, they are special effects with the accent on special.

The lost city of the Amazons is beautifully rendered, with impressive idols and sacred monuments; some are created full size and some as convincing miniatures, featuring perhaps the finest production design of any RKO Tarzan. The film comes tantalizingly close to evoking the magic of an A. Merritt story, lacking only a touch of pulp poetry to lift it above the ordinary (its script is credited to the otherwise undistinguished John Jacoby and Marjorie L. Pfaelzer). It is, however, a little disappointing to note that the Amazons worship stone idols of gods instead of goddesses.

It should be noted here that the RKO *Tarzan*s were never low-budget films, unlike the *Jungle Jim* and *Bomba, the Jungle Boy* movies that would follow. They often sport huge studio settings and crowds of extras. Only a certain lack of care that often crops up marks them as a step down from their predecessors at MGM.

For example, the swarms of Amazons are cute to look at (there's this one curvaceous babe in a white dress who really stands out in the crowd scenes) and are attractively costumed in alternately white and leopard-skin outfits. If you like leg, this is your movie. Unfortunately,

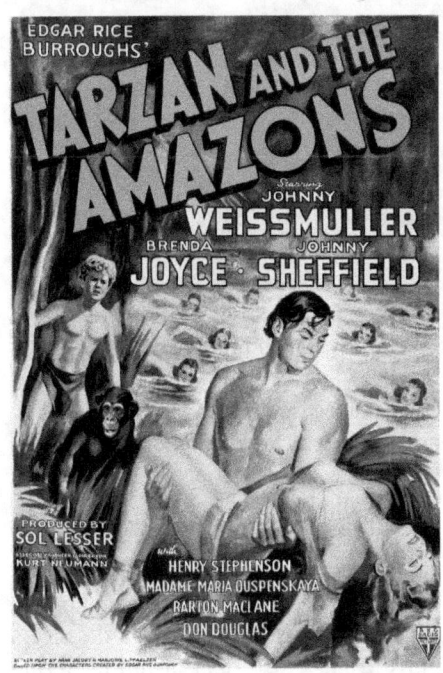

none of those costumes have been draped over actresses of any perceptible skill. In the action scenes they stalk their prey less like Amazonian warriors than like, well, like a bunch of *girls*. If only Kurt Neumann had gotten a couple of real athletes and archers, at least for action shots, to leave us a little less on our own with the ol' suspension of disbelief (it definitely helped 1955's *Son of Sinbad*).

Maria Ouspenskaya, however, is absolutely convincing as the Amazonian matriarch. As she was in *The Wolf Man* (1941) and *Frankenstein Meets the Wolf Man* (1943), this old and frail woman (with little tremble that made me worry she was coming down with Parkinson's) is believably a survivor of a lost age, the guardian of ancient knowledge.

Unfortunately, three minutes after we reach the elaborate lost city of the Amazons, we leave it. And we don't return until the last third of the film. Darn!

Much of the rest of *Tarzan and the Amazons* takes place in the village of Randini, apparently so near the tree house that Tarzan is a familiar figure, making his jungle home appear much less isolated than it had been only a few films before.

Randini contains the first actual black people to be seen in the RKO *Tarzan*s. Indeed, they appear to be the only black people that *ever* appear in the RKO Tarzans. They are employed as native bearers in the safari scenes, and while none of them are granted any actual dialogue, they do have that obligatory jungle movie scene in which they drop their loads and flee in superstitious terror. I should also point out that, in contrast with the more-or-less Caucasian extras that populate the other African locations of RKO, these black bearers are markedly less advanced on the ladder of civilization. Their dress is more primitive. None of them seems able to handle the English language. And their I.Q. scores appear to be several points lower. (Even the bearers of *Tarzan and the Huntress* handle firearms and are allowed wise, articulate leaders.) Well, at least their existence is acknowledged.

I don't want to harp on the subject, but the series' depictions of Africa actually did influence attitudes outside the movie theater. Or as Lorraine Hansberry has a character say in her 1959 Broadway play *A Raisin in the Sun*, "All anyone seems to know about when it comes to Africa is Tarzan." It is probably too much to ask of any work intended to be no more than a popular entertainment that it bear the weight of such heavy cultural responsibility. Except for the fact that they do, whether they want to or not.

The other highlight of *Tarzan and the Amazons* is the much-needed return of Jane. And as the Victory Jane for the rest of this series, Brenda Joyce is way better than we had any right to expect. Ms. Joyce is a decent performer, becoming a good foil for Weissmuller, remaining enjoyable throughout. Her biggest handicap is simply that she isn't Maureen O'Sullivan. Watching her play *house* with Tarzan has the bittersweet quality of having dinner with a dear friend who has married a nice woman, but one who looks just like his first wife.

Brenda Joyce is one of those Hollywood Cinderella stories that make less fortunate actors want to blow their brains out. Depending on what newspaper clipping you happen to find, her original name was Graftina Lebo (Boston Post, 1941), Betty Leaba (*Newsday*, 2009), Betty Liebo (*NY Post*, 1940), Betty Leabo (*Life* Magazine, 1939), Betty Laftina Leabo (*Daily Variety* Gotham, 2009) or Betty ("call me Graftina") Graffina Leabo (IMDb, 2010). By any name she was a pretty co-ed at University of California, L.A., paying her way as a photo model when Daryl Zanuck offered her a screen test and then the starring role in *The Rains Came*. Her performance for that major 20th Century Fox release of 1939 was well received, immediately jump-starting a career as a Hollywood leading lady. Of the 26 films she made between 1939 and 1949, none are classics (*Strange Confession* [1945], *Pillow of Death* [1945], *The Spider Woman Strikes Back* [1946]), but she worked frequently and never once had to play less than third lead; right up to the end she was often first billed. She left the profession at the

The happy family returns to the treehouse. We have the return of Jane (Brenda Joyce), who is reunited with Tarzan, as Boy awakens and stretches at the start of another day.

end of that decade to rejoin the world of anonymous working stiffs, and until her death in 2009, none of her casual friends or co-workers ever suspected her 10-year reign as a movie star.

Jane's reunion with Tarzan fills much of the slow center of *Tarzan and the Amazons*, and while their frolicking among trees and ponds cannot compete with the sheer pre-Code carnality of the early MGM productions, the domestic contentment they exude feels totally in line with the evolving affections of any long-lasting marriage. Especially after kids intervene.

More running time is filled up with Boy's growing pains and the usual Cheetah clowning. And fortunately endearing moments of character development occur. Do you want to know what character development is? In a fatherly moment in *Tarzan Triumphs*, the jungle lord admonishes his adopted son, saying, "Tarzan know best for Boy. Tarzan mother now." And then he playfully kicks Boy in the butt. In *Amazons*, when Boy expresses relief that Jane is back to do the cooking again, the jungle lord admits, "Tarzan bad mother. Good father." And then playfully kicks Boy in the butt. That is what character development is.

In Kurt Neumann's second entry, *Tarzan and the Leopard Woman* (1946), civilization intrudes into the jungle. Some pretty, fair-skinned young ladies from the local "Zambesi School" who we would today call student interns are sent to set up a school in the "territory of Bergandi." This example of what we would today call cultural imperialism has, according to Bergandi leader Lazar (Edgar Barrier), "reduced the proud people of Zambesi to a race of sniveling shopkeepers ..." Lazar is "partially native" (never a good sign) and leads a group of what I suppose we would today call a cult of leopard fundamentalists who dress up in leopard skins to commit various acts of what we would today call terrorism.

The leopard guys are really cool, with their leopard-skin masks and capes and Wolverine claws (I wish I had a set for Halloween), and they inspire a couple of legitimately scary moments.

In one remarkable long shot, two of those Zambesi teachers run towards the camera, pursued by two leopard dudes. One girl trips and is grabbed, the other glances back over her shoulder and then she resumes running toward us. (Between her and the camera hang a couple of leaves and branches, conveying to us the dense jungle into which she hopes to escape.) Just as she is about to reach us, two leopard men leap into the left and right sides of the frame to seize her. They enter with their clawed hands upraised, so the first things we see enter the frame are their claws in super close-up. The composition and blocking of that one shot shows more forethought and creativity than just about any moment in any RKO *Tarzan*. I'm sure it got screams from the audience. It deserves to be in a better movie than this one.

The leopard men indulge in several ritual dance sequences, usually the low point of "lost race" movies, and I have to say the actors do a damn good job. Their climactic dance is beautifully staged. They dance in a circle around a campfire, banging drums. The camera is set at waist level just outside the circle, so in the background the leopard dancers move from left to right in full flickering firelight, while in the foreground leopard dancers move from right to left in black silhouettes. They do a lot of energetic leaping, the aggressively masculine sort of choreography that Gene Kelly mastered to keep the sight of dancing men from ever looking unmanly.

The leopard guys are some of the few decent jungle fighters that Weissmuller encounters in his cinematic career, and the body count the jungle lord runs up is surprisingly high, making the action sequences in *Leopard Woman* probably the most exciting of the RKO Tarzans.

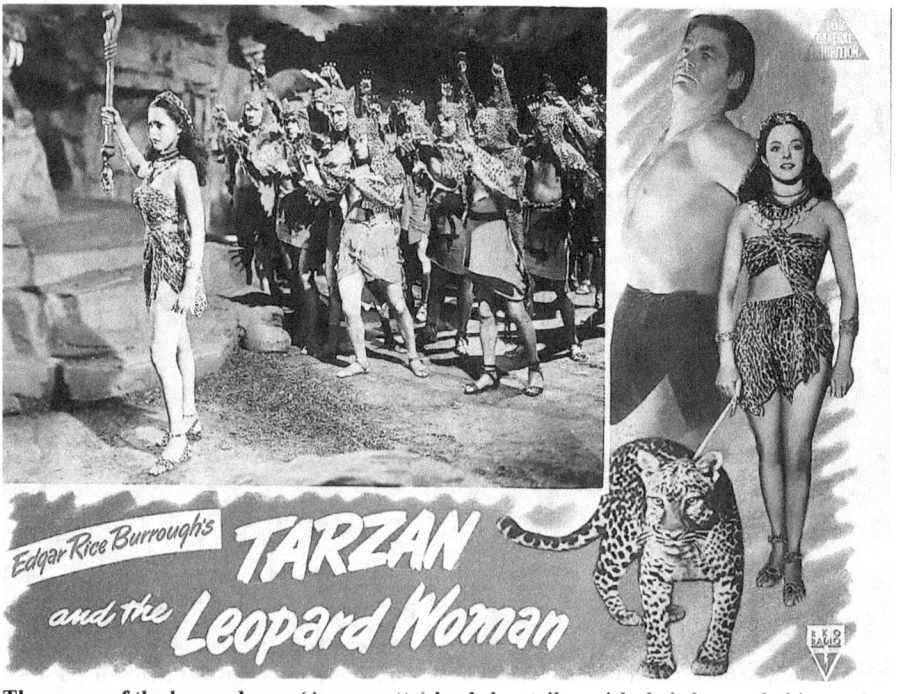

The queen of the leopard men (Acquanetta) leads her tribe, with their leopard-skin masks, capes and Wolverine claws.

Though I am disappointed that *not once* does Tarzan triumphantly call out his jungle yell.

A leopard boy named Kimba (Tommy Cook) turns up who is anxious to prove himself a leopard man by killing someone in the cult's name. He insinuates himself into Tarzan and Jane's tree house by pretending to be a leopard refugee, all the while itching to assert his manhood by killing Jane, all by himself. He doesn't seem to have to walk all that far to get from Bergandi to the tree house.

As Kimba, Tommy Cook is really creepy. I mean, that kid is evil, truly bloodthirsty, giving an actual taste of the feral kids used in dirty little wars to this day. It is a little annoying that Jane, after coping in the jungle for years, proves herself so useless in fighting him off. And that Kimba doesn't meet his deserved end in a climactic battle with Boy.

Tarzan and the Leopard Woman is probably the most entertaining of the RKO *Tarzan*s, though for my taste not quite as much fun as *Tarzan and the Amazons*, being less of a scientific romance and consequently showing off fewer special effects (until a climax, which actually does give a modest reminder of the company that created *King Kong*).

I haven't even gotten around to the best part of the film. And that is the queen of the leopard men, played by Acquanetta.

All my movie-fan life, I have heard people rhapsodize about the allure of Acquanetta. She talked about a slinky walk she used to attract attention when entering hotel lobbies. For my money, though, no movie of hers has ever conveyed that appeal. Even in her signature film *Captive Wild Woman* (a personal favorite of mine), she has never gotten my hormones racing. Now that I have watched *Tarzan and the Leopard Woman*, however, I now see the light.

Early in the film Acquanetta wears a white dress. It is sheer; it is soft, pulled tight against her skin with no sign of undergarments. I'm sorry, but for a 1940s kids film, that dress is downright pornographic. The fabric is so clinging that she is for all rational purposes frontally nude. When she turns into profile, the sight of her pointy silhouette had me leaning into the TV and shaking violently. Based on this evidence, I can only speculate that in person the woman must have been overpowering. (Late in the film she wears a cute leopard-skin outfit, but for me, it doesn't cut the muster like that white number.)

(Now, before reading this next paragraph, please understand that I love Acquanetta and found her an absolute darling when I finally got to meet her at FANEX [thanks to Gary and Sue Svehla] back in the 1990s. But there is no denying that the woman was a terrible actress. In *Leopard Woman*, however, she is completely competent, almost good. Not once is she actually embarrassing (see *Jungle Woman*, *The Lost Continent*, *Dead Man's Eyes*). This may well be the finest performance Acquanetta ever gave.)

I wouldn't want anyone going in with any excessive expectations. Trust me, if audiences expect to see *The Naked Prey* (1966, a great jungle movie that is also a great movie), they will be disappointed. However, audiences who enjoy sitting with a studio jungle movie like PRC's

Johnny Weissmuller as Tarzan and Johnny Sheffield as Boy, now obviously a young man

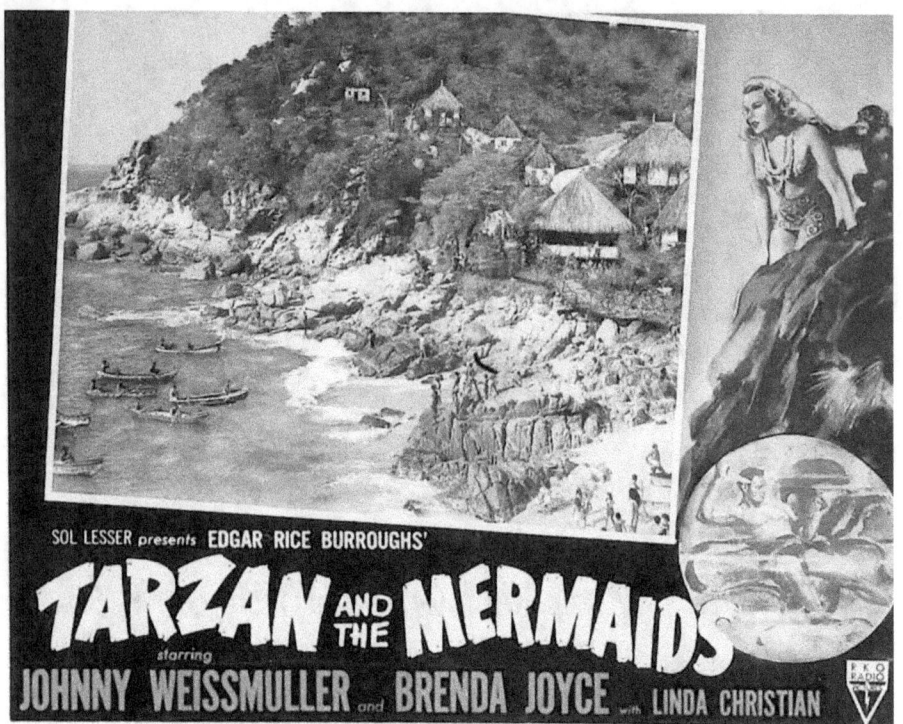

This lobby card shows the steep stone cliffs where the mer-people make their spectacular dives in the movie's jaw-dropping sequence.

White Pongo (1945) will find *Tarzan and the Leopard Woman* pure pleasure. Though by any studio that white dress is star-level stuff.

Kurt Neumann ends his association with Weissmuller with *Tarzan and the Huntress* (1947, though he would direct Lex Baxter in 1953's *Tarzan and the She-Devil*). While its title would make one expect it to be more babe-oriented, as indeed do the titles of all the Neumann *Tarzan*s, *Huntress* is in fact a homey, domestic story. When an expedition comes to trap animals for Western zoos, Tarzan launches a crusade to keep them free.

Tarzan and the Huntress is a kinder, gentler adventure after the bloodbath of *Tarzan and the Leopard Woman*. The change is so great it makes me wonder if protests arose from parents' groups, for the new film is very family-friendly. *Huntress* is not a bad film. It's kind of sweet to see Tarzan as the defender of wildlife, saying lines like, "Animals belong in jungle, not in cages." There's some cute business with a lioness and her cubs, but for my taste this is the least involving of the Kurt Neumann *Tarzan*s. Had he gotten bored with the series (after only three episodes)?

The film's greatest and genuinely poignant interest comes from the fact that it is our last opportunity to see our jungle family together. They enjoy life in their safer, tamer jungle, miles from the deathtrap of *Tarzan and His Mate*, but not far from the nearest village, bridged not by a steep escarpment, but by an easily swimmable river. On that river we see Tarzan, Jane and Boy swim in unison together, stroke-by-stroke. That image is a pretty good metaphor for their perfectly harmonious, balanced family relationship. Mirroring them, even Cheetah has adopted a family.

But things are on the verge of change. From the very first time we see him and hear his suddenly deeper voice, Boy is obviously now a young man. One of Tarzan's first lines is, "Boy a man now, do man's work." We see them indulge in some endearing father-son rivalry in which Tarzan good-naturedly shows Boy his place with a high-spirited, "Boy not big enough for Tarzan yet!"

However, when their animal friends have been caged and important work has to be done, for the first time in the series the two men of the Tarzan household go together to set them free. And when their work is done, Tarzan puts an arm proudly over his man-child's shoulder as they go. In his pride there seems no shadow to suggest that his son will not always be there by his side.

And so we turn to the last of the RKO *Tarzan*s starring Johnny Weissmuller, *Tarzan and the Mermaids* (1948). the movie has a number of strengths, though few of them involve Tarzan himself. It is in many ways less a sequel than an afterthought to Weissmuller's Tarzan films.

Things have changed even over the opening credits, where we discover that this was not shot at RKO but photographed instead on location and at a studio in Mexico.

Long gone are the days when the family tree house was located on an inaccessible escarpment surrounded by deadly pigmies, cannibals and savage apes. Nope, now Tarzan and Jane reside so near to civilization that family friends casually drop by to say hello. The entire opening of the film concerns a man called Benji, who stops by to deliver the mail and sing a few songs (not only was the film made in Mexico, but in many ways it feels like a Mexican popcorn film).

The sleepy domesticity of the Tarzan household is interrupted by the arrival of a maiden fleeing a lost city of fishermen/pearl divers. Tarzan offers her sanctuary at his tree house just before some of her fellow worshipers drag her home to be wed to the living personification of their god. Enraged, Tarzan and Jane

follow them to the lost city where they … become tourists. That's right, tourists. They hang around on the beaches, eating and watching the natives at their quaint games and native rituals.

The film features extensive location work at Aztec ruins and on the beautiful beaches of Acapulco. In fact, much of the film feels like a travelogue paid for by the Acapulco Tourist Board, complete with picturesque voice-over narration. I suspect that Weissmuller and Joyce had a great time making the film, but as an action/adventure epic, it leaves something to be desired.

Shooting in Mexico gives director Robert Florey (*The Coconuts* [1929], *Murders in the Rue Morgue* [1932], *The Beast With Five Fingers* [1946]) incredible resources, including elaborate sets adorning the already-magnificent locations populated by huge numbers of extras, and a welcome return of those Weissmuller swimming scenes shot underwater.

Still, much missed is the RKO special effects department. No matte paintings appear, except for stock footage of the tree house which doesn't resemble the set built for this film, and a couple of times still photographs of caverns are used (fairly effectively) in place of paintings.

We are told that Boy has gone to college, and their father-son interaction is sorely missed. Well, realistically, how long was the kid going to stick around a neighborhood where the only girl was his Mom? Also missing is the Cheetah of old. After seeing *Tarzan and the Mermaids*, I take back every bad thing I ever said about Cheetah. There is some new chimp in this movie that is so inexpressive that, I can't believe I'm saying this, I began to miss the skill and personality the previous Cheetahs brought to the series.

Classic movie bad guy George Zucco is in there somewhere, but he doesn't do very much. Tarzan defeats him by employing a complex understanding of societal relationships more appropriate to the Lone Ranger than to the lord of the apes.

Tarzan and the Mermaids does have one absolutely jaw-dropping sequence. Among the various recreational activities that the smiling jungle lord and his mate watch is a ritual or sporting event in which the mer-people dive off steep stone

Tarzan and Jane (Brenda Joyce) are victims of the lost city of fishermen/pearl divers and the living personification of their god.

cliffs that go right down into the sea. They dive in groups; they dive as individuals; they dive in formations. With each new dive we rise higher and higher up the primordial cliffs, until the sequence takes on an absolutely elemental power as their near-naked bodies gracefully sail past the rocks and into the sea like young gods of earth, air and water.

This sequence would be one of the high points in the cinematic annals of Tarzan if only this scene had something to do with the *plot* of the damned film. Come on, was there really no way to incorporate this scene into the narrative, to meld it into the actual action of the movie? Couldn't the mer-people be leaping from the cliffs to stop Tarzan as he escapes or swims to save his mate? Or something? Alas, the script by Carroll Young (who has story credits on all the RKO *Tarzan*s and who would go on to write lots of *Jungle Jim* features) shows very little feel for the mythology of Tarzan. So little that Tarzan is barely in his own movie. Hell, I don't think he uses his jungle yell even once.

So ends the last of the Weissmuller *Tarzan*s. Future adapters of Edgar Rice Burroughs' greatest creation would pick up the practice of shooting on location and use such locales to greater effect.

These RKO *Tarzan*s were never great films. Some of them aren't even good, especially if one happens to live at the wrong end of racial politics. Burroughs himself may have regarded them as a necessary evil to keep his creation's name in the spotlight, but these movies do not disgrace the memory of the couple and then trio created at MGM in the 1930s, with whom the whole world fell in love. And for all the mean-spirited remarks that have been made over the years, this star, to the day he hung up his shorts, looked damn good for a 40-something man.

At the age of 46, Johnny Weissmuller left for, well, I can't exactly say fresher pastures, but at least the familiar thrills of the *Jungle Jim* series at Columbia. Like a miniature version of his adoptive dad, Johnny Sheffield would get his own, smaller series, as *Bomba, the Jungle Boy*, for Monogram. Brenda Joyce would return to the family tree house one more time, in *Tarzan's Magic Fountain* (1949), but this time with a younger, more muscular jungle mate (who'd thought she had it in her?). Both Sheffield and Joyce lived to the end of their lives in California. Weissmuller's last years were spent in Mexico, not far from the *Tarzan and the Mermaids* locations where his lord of the jungle seemed so content.

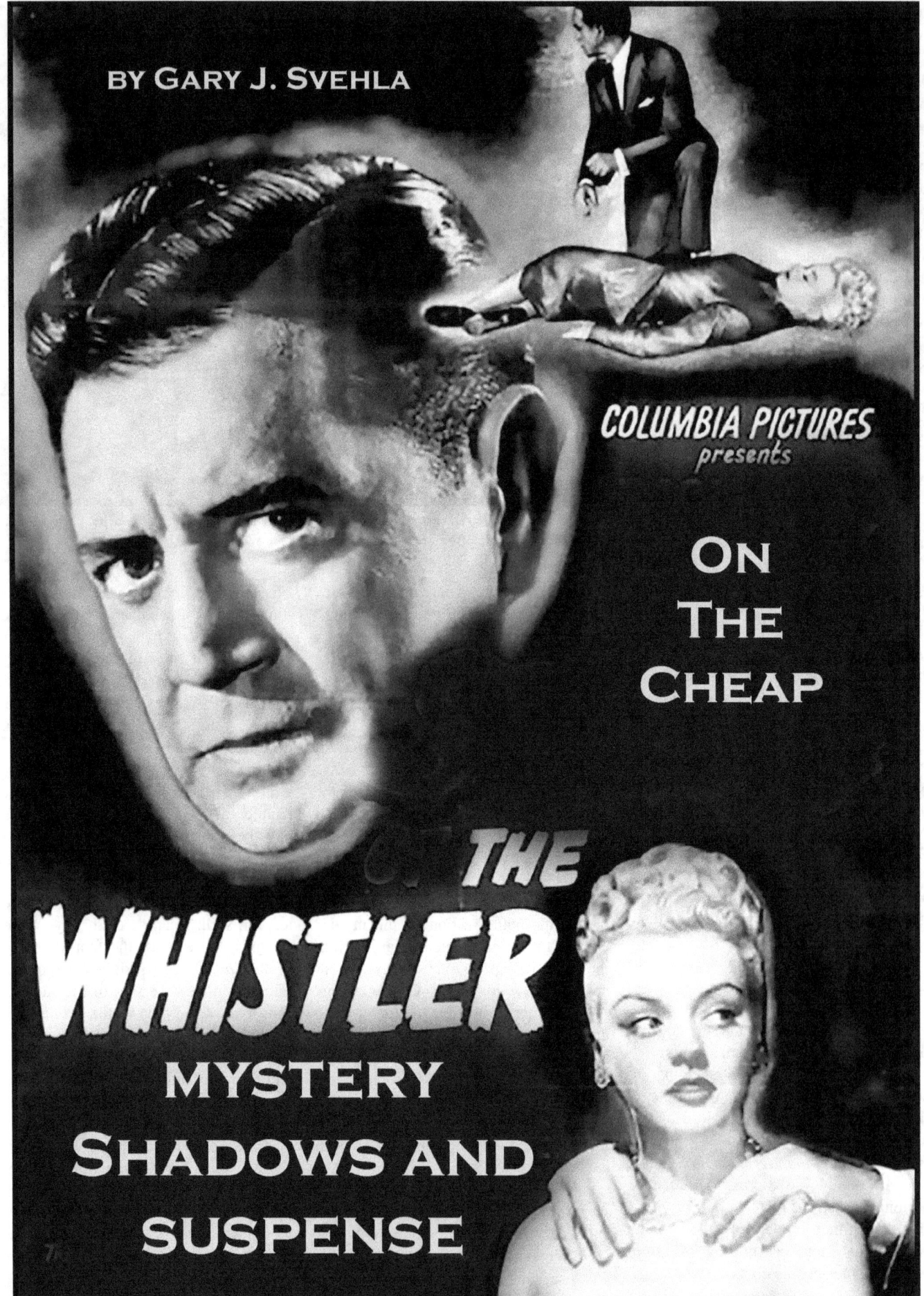

Turner Classic Movies must be commended for unearthing B-crime movie series that usually screen on Saturday mornings. The more familiar series shown include *The Saint* and *The Falcon*, while lesser-known ones include *Boston Blackie*, *The Lone Wolf* and *The Crime Club*. But among my favorite B-crime series is *The Whistler*, a collection of eight Columbia movies released between 1944 and 1948. Based upon the popular radio series that ran from May 1942 through July 1955 over CBS' West Coast network, the series' calling call was an eerie 13-note musical theme (composed by Wilbur Hatch) whistled by Dorothy Roberts. Bill Forman starred in the title role on radio through most of its run, and he also narrated the Columbia films. The originally un-credited (to create an air of mystery) actor who portrayed the Whistler on screen was Otto Forrest. The Whistler on radio mimicked another radio powerhouse (straight from the majesty of the pulps), the Shadow, and both series are similar yet different. The Shadow became the crime-fighting hero who emerged front and center. He was the dark-cloaked hero who clouded men's minds and solved the mystery. The Whistler, on the other hand, lurks in the shadows, narrates psychological undercurrents, interprets actions and advances the plot for the protagonist. But he remains generally a narrator and observer, and he rarely intervenes in the action. Instead he serves as the moral compass of each story.

This Columbia B-movie series often echoed the tenants of film noir—shadowy, dark photography; basically decent people who are caught in moral anguish and criminals who get so immersed in a corrupt universe that death is often the only way out. The radio and movie series opened with the introductory words of the Whistler: "I am the Whistler. I know many things, for I walk by night. I know many strange tales, many secrets, hidden in the hearts of men and women, who have stepped into the shadows. Yes, I know the nameless terrors of which they dare not speak." The character of the Whistler serves much like Alfred Hitchcock did on *Alfred Hitchcock Presents* or Boris Karloff on his *Thriller* TV series ... he served as the fictional host of a dark-themed anthology series

The disheveled Conrad (Richard Dix) awakens in the abandoned warehouse to find himself almost clubbed to death for his money, from *The Whistler*.

where different characters face life's darkest demons, episode after episode. All of the eight movies run about one hour long, and William Castle directed half of them. Of course, the more mature Castle would skyrocket to fame, over a decade later, with his series of gimmick-laden horror/suspense movies, including *Macabre, House on Haunted Hill, The Tingler* and *13 Ghosts*. But the better *Whistler* entries shine because of their shimmering cinematography and imaginative direction. Richard Dix (the star of Val Lewton's *The Ghost Ship*) starred in seven of the eight entries, playing a multitude of different roles. He gave the anthology B-series a consistency and identifiable B-star presence. He never played the same role twice, but his voice and face came to be identified with the series.

The Whistler, the debuting feature released by Columbia in 1944, screenplay by Eric Taylor, cinematography by James S. Brown, directed by William Castle, features Richard Dix as Earl Conrad, a man of means, waiting for the arrival of his contact while he sits in a seedy, wharf-side bar. As the Whistler informs us, "The man sitting alone is a stranger here ... He is a man who is more at home at a fashionable club than a waterfront bar. But tonight he has turned from the comfort and security in his own world to meet a man whose business is death!" The man who deals in death is shady Lefty Vigran (Don Costello), a hit-man manager who works out of Bill Tomley's Bail Bonds office. Conrad pays Vigran $10,000 to kill a man, whose name and address he writes on a card and passes to Vigran. Conrad tells Vigran the job must be done by next Friday night. Vigran says he does not do the actual job but works with a man who does. Vigran tells Conrad that the actual shooter will not know Conrad and that Conrad won't know the shooter, to protect both parties.

The element of twist and surprise enters when we learn that Earl Conrad is arranging his own death. His wife apparently died when the Japanese attacked the cruise ship on which the couple traveled, Conrad attempting a last-ditch effort to patch up his deteriorating marriage. Despondent with the implication hanging around him that he allowed his wife to die, Conrad wants to end his life.

J. Carrol Naish plays the reclusive and low-key nameless killer. First seen reading a book on necrophobia (the exaggerated fear of death) while a delivery boy slips the killer $5,000 cash under his rooming house door, the professional reads the card with the name and address

of his victim and burns it. Naish plays an unemotional, totally professional killer, but his ability to lurk in the shadows and be unseen makes his presence appear almost supernatural. Naish is steely cool and unassuming, quite literally a man who could fade into the woodwork until, like a hidden snake, he strikes.

The psychological subplot involves Conrad opening up his wounded psyche to his personal secretary, Alice Walker (Gloria Stuart of *The Invisible Man*), about how he abandoned his friends who knew that he and his wife were experiencing difficulties, perhaps anticipating a separation. When he returned home after the reconciliation cruise ended tragically, many eyebrows were raised. Conrad tells Alice how he helped many people onto the life raft, but these same friends wondered why Earl could not save his own wife. Of course Alice blatantly loves Earl but Earl is too wrapped up in his own problems to notice.

In a clever sequence the shooter, announcing himself as Smith, calls on Conrad at his ceramic manufacturing office, under the false pretense of selling him life insurance (very ironic considering "Mr. Smith" is the hit man hired to kill Conrad). Using the hard sell, Smith tells Conrad no one knows how long anyone has or knows what might be awaiting him or her around the next corner. Smith even paints a picture of Conrad having a fire at his home and suffocating to death as a result. "What makes you so sure that nothing unexpected will ever happen to you?" Smith asks. Smith's final words to Conrad, "I'll see you around sometime," ring both sinisterly and matter-of-factly at the same time. Obviously, the killer wanted to have the advantage of getting close to Conrad, to play a little game of cat-and-mouse before the shooting. Smith enjoys the hunt as much as the kill.

In very suspenseful sequence, Conrad returns home after dark to find that someone has broken his front glass window. Just as he enters the house, anticipating a break-in, a telephone repairman sneaks up behind him to repair his out-of-order phone (after dark, after office hours and Conrad has not even placed a service repair call). Allowing the gruff repairman into his home (believing him to be the hit man), they both discover that the phone cable has been cut. But lurking in the shadows of the adjacent room is J. Carrol Naish, who awaits the perfect opportunity to do his job. When he is ready to strike, Alice Walker just happens to drop by (again, after dark, unexpected). The killer exits by the back door but takes careful aim at Conrad while lurking outside his large front window, but Alice's closeness does not allow the professional a clean shot. The sudden appearance of the shadow of the Whistler and his 13-note calling card musical cue disrupts the killer, who gives up and flees. Alice asks, "Did you hear someone whistling?" In the next sequence J. Carrol Naish returns home to his apartment to find an old friend there, Gorman (Alan Dinehart), a man who wants the killer to take a vacation trip with him. Naish explains to Gorman that he has a job to do for Lefty Vigran, that he feels nervous because of a presence watching him—and whistling! In a very revealing line, the killer slowly gripes, "I've been paid, I've got to deliver," demonstrating his ethics as a paid, professional killer.

Alice, in the ironic course of events, delivers a telegram to Conrad from the American Red Cross revealing that his wife is alive and being held prisoner by the Japanese. And when Conrad attempts to track down Lefty Vigran to call off the hit man, he learns that Vigran has been shot dead by the police and no one knows his partner's identity. Conrad now wants to live but has no way to call off the hit.

Things get creepier when the disheveled Conrad (who survived a fatal car crash) goes to a flop house and buys a bed for a quarter, but when Conrad wakes up the next morning to leave, it turns out his stalker has been sleeping several beds away the entire night, watching over him. A down-on-his-luck man convinces Conrad to go with him to a deserted warehouse to spend the night safely. However, when Conrad settles down on a pile of old newspapers there, the man tries to club Conrad to death for his money. But Naish's unseen bullet saves Conrad's life ... momentarily.

J. Carrol Naish tells his buddy that he is dedicated to finishing his job, that his reputation means everything and that he takes pride in delivering on his promise and payment. In contrast, Conrad, having marital problems, is seen in a negative light by his friends and lives in fear of disgrace. That ends when his wife turns up alive as a prisoner. J. Carrol Naish, on the one hand, is a professional killer who has a strong sense of business ethnics. Conrad, on the other hand, finds himself criticized by his own business partner who is upset over Conrad's infrequent visits to the office of late. In many ways Naish's sense of responsibility and pride in his work outshines Conrad's. Naish even admits to having too much fun in his "job" to leave town. The killer calls his stalking of his victim (where the victim senses he is being stalked) his psychological experiment and seems to be enjoying the hell out of it. "They tell me it's hard on the nerves," the killer declares. Naish delivers his lines almost in a whisper with quiet intensity. He smiles with self-satisfaction. Naish refers to Conrad as his little playmate.

By this time Conrad is sleep deprived looking rather like hell, living and sleeping in the same clothes, on the run

Earl Conrad, a man of means, slowly becomes unhinged as he realizes that the man he hired to kill him takes the responsibilities of his job very seriously, from *The Whistler*.

from Naish. The two ultimately meet up in a little restaurant dive and Conrad spills his guts, giving Naish the facts, wanting to call off the hit and allowing Naish to keep all the money. But when Conrad mentions he knows that Naish shot and killed the derelict in the warehouse, Naish utters something about Conrad knowing too much to live.

In the film's final suspenseful minutes, Conrad attempts to stowaway aboard a Red Cross ship as Naish attempts to sneak into the wharf watchman's shack where Conrad was residing. When Conrad is recognized and detained in the shipping office, the clever Naish takes dead aim from outside the office window, but ominous whistling distracts him. A shot rings out that goes wild, but the fleeing Naish is shot and killed. The Whistler tells us, "It was this man's destiny to die this night. Earl Conrad lives! ... You cannot change your destiny. I know because I am—the Whistler!" The Whistler, cloaked in black, returns to the shadows as the end credits appear.

This initial *Whistler* entry contains all the strengths that make the series memorable. We have two psychologically damaged characters, with perhaps the killer J. Carrol Naish the mentally healthier of the two. Conrad is the morally conflicted individual who weighs the worth of his own life in the shadow of disgrace and aspersions cast that he allowed his own wife to die. Into this environment comes moody and dark photography that heightens the suspense and fear factor. The narrator, the Whistler, becomes an overseer and appears during crucial times to interpret what is occurring psychologically in our protagonist's mind. In the best entries the supporting cast is always excellent and helps to make the character created by Richard Dix seem real. The tone of each entry is sometimes ironic, sometimes somber, at other times simply clever and suspenseful, but each entry is always ominous and bathes characters in shades of deadly shadows. *The Whistler* sets the bar high.

William Castle directed the second entry in the series, *The Mark of the Whistler*, released in 1944 by Columbia, from a screenplay by George Bricker, based upon a Cornell Woolrich (the author who wrote *Rear Window*, among many other classics) story. George Meehan handles cinematography, but he was not required to generate the shadowy noir textures of the first entry. While *The Mark of the Whistler* is solidly entertaining, it lacks the suspense, fear factor and ambience of paranoia that made *The Whistler* so excellent. For me irony and plot twists cannot make up for the missing aspects from the first entry. Still, *The Mark of the Whistler* is very

childhood home to a vacant lot, where 20 years earlier, a fire destroyed an apartment building. Several members of the other Nugent family were killed, including Lee's mother. The father had already moved to South America, fleeing the country because of criminal charges placed against him involving the business he co-owned. Young Lee Nugent was only 12 and made a ward of the state and ultimately adopted, but he ran away three years later and was never heard from again. In order to put this fabrication across, the down-on-his-luck Lee Nugent learns all the names and dates to convince the bank that he is the rightful owner of the account.

Penniless and without a clean suit to his name, Lee Nugent goes to a store and enlists the owner Joe Sorsby (Porter Hall) to front him the money for a room, food and a new suit of clothes. For his efforts Nugent promises to pay the man back double. In a delightful performance, Porter Hall plays Sorsby, droopy glasses and even droopier long cigar dangling in his mouth, as a prissy and sneaky entrepreneur who calls everyone "brother" yet trusts no one. Even when Nugent goes to the bank, Sorsby insists he tag along, and when Nugent makes him stand across the street to wait, Sorsby assures him that he will keep his eyes peeled on the door. The bank manager needs to see documentation that Nugent is Nugent, and when the now well-dressed derelict cannot produce much more than a social security card, he has to submit to an interrogation where he gets to use all his recently learned facts. A few days later Nugent is told the money will be released to him. Not knowing the amount in the account, Nugent is shaken when he learns he will be handed a little over $29,000 in cash. In one of the film's best sequences, as Nugent awaits the arrival of the money, he sits alone inside the bank office cubicle and watches the bank guard and (panning left to right) every teller look suspiciously at him, and for the first time Nugent begins to sweat and look nervous. Seldom has total paranoia been captured so well in 1940s cinema. And all the quick cuts showing people staring at him are filmed at high angle, looking down at the diminutive crook. The Whistler, always in time of psychological stress, adds a narrative aside. "What did he mean when he told you *not* to go away. Will he come back with the *money* or a *detective*? Everyone in the place seems to be staring at *you*, waiting, it's still not *too late* for

entertaining and achieves high marks. It remains one of the better entries of the series.

Star Richard Dix, however, might be even more satisfying here as Lee Selfredge Nugent, a formerly affluent businessman whose star has fallen and now he is a homeless derelict. As the Whistler tells the audience, "I knew him in better days when he possessed money, power, influence; but fate decreed that those material things should slip away and that I, the Whistler, should find him tonight, alone on this park bench. What can the future hold for a man like this?"

Basically the hour-long B-feature divides into halves. The half deals with Lee Nugent's scam. He reads a newspaper ad for dormant accounts at the local bank, and one of these long-neglected accounts is waiting to be claimed by a Lee Nugent. Of course not Lee S. Nugent, but another man named Lee Nugent. Doing his homework, Lee traces the other Nugent's

"Don't be frightened. We just want your picture for the paper!"

Lee Nugent (Richard Dix) dodges pretty newspaper reporter Pat Henley (Janis Carter) and accidentally bumps into street peddler Limpy Smith (Paul Guilfoyle).

you to change your mind!" The camera frames Nugent's moist face in close-up, the man's darting eyes telegraphing his guilt and fear. But when the bank manager returns, Nugent almost blows the scheme by signing his middle name on the release form, remembering quickly that the other Nugent had no middle name. A quick fountain pen smudge saves the day, as he pockets $29,000 in cash and nervously leaves the bank. Outside Nugent, dazzled and disoriented by Pat Henley (Janis Carter), a pretty female newspaper reporter, he dodges the photographer's camera, not wishing to be identified. In the confusion Nugent bumps into equally poor street peddler Limpy Smith (Paul Guilfoyle), whose stark lingering stare at Nugent foreshadows this character's increasing importance. But Limpy is very friendly and helpful to Nugent, especially after he gets a 10 spot from Nugent for any damages his bump may have caused. Sorsby is out of the picture after Nugent shoves him a $100 bill.

Now begins the second half with Nugent's elation and then increasing nervousness over his crime. Another sordid and stereotypical gangster type, identified as Eddie Donnelly (John Calvert), enters the scene as he buys a newspaper and eyeballs Lee Nugent's photo. Even before Donnelly says or does anything, the audience realizes that he is a villain and a man to avoid at all cost. He mutters to himself that he will kill Nugent and returns to his home to tell piano-playing brother Perry (Matt Willis, the man who played the werewolf in *Return of the Vampire*) the news.

In a most suspenseful sequence, Nugent dines alone in luxury but soon spots cute newspaper reporter Pat Henley and invites her to his table. Soon the ominous Donnelly appears, who sits a few tables away, sizing up Nugent. Nugent suspects Donnelly is a detective, perhaps hired by the bank to tail him. Desperate to exit without being followed, Nugent pretends to go to the bathroom and bribes the black attendant to sneak him out (in this case an exit window hidden behind a framed painting). Donnelly, threatening the same attendant with violence, escapes through the same exit. Nugent, slithering down deserted dark side streets, hears the Whistler's theme and sees his silhouette. But only the audience hears his narration, introduced with a little laugh. "This is an amazing turn of events, Lee Nugent … Now you are hunted. Is it by someone who knows of the fraud you perpetrated?" And then the shadow disappears. Limpy Smith intercepts Nugent to tell him that two rough looking guys were grilling the doorman at his hotel. Limpy tells him that one of the two men had a crazy look in his eyes and swore he was going to get Nugent. In this wonderful encounter, Limpy, wearing a floppy hat, is totally covered by the shadows of night (it's only the hat that we can see to identify Limpy's voice echoing from beneath it, and once in a while the light reflects and sparkles off his eyes), speaking to Nugent who stands equally accented by dark shadows that cover his face. This sequence contains the best cinematography of the entire movie. Limpy suggests Nugent escape town by bus that leaves at midnight from the terminal. Nugent knows that Limpy has access to the service elevators and asks him to sneak into his room and fetch a metal tin hidden inside his icebox. Nugent promises to pay him $50 when the box is delivered at the bus station.

In the next sequence, the gimpy Limpy finds the metal tin box, but its lid flips open to reveal a pile of money. Meanwhile Donnelly arrives outside Nugent's room, listening for any movement inside and waits in the shadows as Limpy exits. Of course Limpy is followed to the bus station. Limpy arrives

Lee Nugent bends down to meet the semi-comatose Donnelly father, the original business partner of the *other* Lee Nugent. The sons of Donnelly (standing left) are Perry (Matt Willis) and Eddie (John Calvert).

to deliver the box and states he saw the $28,000 inside. Nugent seems shocked that Limpy did not take the money and run, but Limpy says he thinks of Nugent as a friend and advises his pal to board the bus immediately. Limpy's parting words to Nugent are that he lives at 410 Pocono Street #8, if Nugent ever needs help. Limpy repeats the address several times for emphasis. Unfortunately, when Limpy leaves, Donnelly arrives, flashes a detective's badge and puts Nugent in handcuffs, citing the case of a policeman killed in Chicago (the same line delivered in the first *Whistler* entry). Fortunately Pat Henley sees this action coming down from a safe distance and phones the police for help. Of course the Donnelly brothers are not detectives and they take Nugent back to their house. In an ironic plot development, the brothers reveal themselves to be the sons of a semi-comatose father, who they wheel out; the man happens to be the business partner of the *other* Lee Nugent. It seems Nugent was conducting illegal business and fled the country, leaving the elder Donnelly holding the bag (even though he was innocent). Serving a long prison sentence, the elder Donnelly's mind snapped and now the Donnelly sons want revenge for their father. Of course Lee S. Nugent protests and pleads that he is not *that* Lee Nugent. But the Donnelly boys believe they got the right man and all three go for a fatal ride. Donnelly enjoys telling Nugent how he will make him die very slowly. "You will die all right, but your mind will go first!" Suddenly the car runs into a street closure, and guess what, it just happens to be Pocono Street. Backing up, Donnelly's car is rear-ended and Nugent makes a run for his life, hoping to find Limpy's apartment. When Nugent finds Limpy, the script's greatest implausibility occurs when Limpy reveals that he is the actual Lee Nugent, the man the Donnelly brothers are after. The police just happen to arrive on the scene when the Donnelly boys are trying to break into the apartment and Eddie is shot and killed.

In the film's final hospital scene, Lee Nugent recovers when the legitimate Lee Nugent (Limpy) states he will not press charges against the criminal Nugent, but, unfortunately, the bank definitely will. That means the derelict Nugent will have to serve jail time for his crime of fraud. Pan Henley, smiling and standing by the bed, states she will wait for him. And in the final irony, Limpy reveals that after he found the $28,000 in the icebox he deposited the money in his bank account, so the money was perfectly safe in the rightful owner's possession. Limpy wants to start up a new business and hire on the fraudulent Nugent as a partner, calling the firm Nugent & Nugent. At this point amid smiles and well wishes by all, the Whistler's calling card is again heard. "Lee Nugent … learned the hard way that there is no compromise with conscience. After he pays that debt to society, fate will be kinder to him. I know because—I am the Whistler!"

Lacking the cat-and-mouse stalker-prey suspense of *The Whistler*, *The Mark of the Whistler* relies upon irony, plot twists and deception, demonstrating how the deceiver is deceived. Call it poetic justice, but Richard Dix's performance as the conflicted Nugent is calm and reserved at first, but soon paranoia and fear takes over as Nugent becomes engulfed in a terrifying world created by his own criminal decisions. What makes the film work so well is the total likability created by Dix in his performance. He becomes the down-on-his-luck *everyman* who makes a bad choice, but soon realizes his error. But with a job and beautiful blonde waiting for him, and the Whistler even promising that fate will be kinder to Nugent, how can the film *not* end more optimistically than it does? The script is filled with intensity, suspense and a sense that the sky is falling down upon Lee S. Nugent. For a B-programmer, *The Mark of the Whistler* distinguishes itself.

These first two *Whistler* productions set the bar high for the remainder of

(left to right): Jean Lang (Janis Carter, who played Pat the newspaper reporter in the last entry), Charlie Kent (Loren Tindall) and Jean's sister Francie (Jeff Donnell) play gin in a Greenwich Village bar/restuarant and observe the people around them, from *The Power of the Whistler*.

the B-series, and as could be suspected, the series did not always rise as high artistically. But the third one was one of the best. William Castle was out as director and the dependable Lew Landers (director of 1935's *The Raven*) was in. *The Power of the Whistler*, released in 1945, featured a screenplay by Aubrey Wisberg and cinematography by L.W. O'Connell. Richard Dix plays a strange man, William Everest, who starts out as the mirror image of Conrad or Nugent, his shy kindness and politeness dominating. But for the first time Dix plays a thoroughly disturbed, evil man who cannot be redeemed, not even by the Whistler's shadowy intervention.

Director Landers starts off with a marvelous beginning. Pre-credits show the shadow of the Whistler walking down an even darker street, whistling as he goes. After the credits end, in front of a solid light gray backdrop, the shadow of the Whistler delivers his usual opening narration walking closer and closer to the camera, growing larger in size. Then we cut to the Richard Dix character walking down a street, the shadow of the Whistler added optically to the scene and delivering his narration walking behind Dix, (although looking noticeably smaller). These introductory graphics shine.

"Here is a strange man formed in God's image, according to the Bible. But how far is image from mirage? This man looks like all of us, but what separates him from his fellows? It cannot be seen by the naked eye. His name is William Everest, a man with a ghastly mission, which will not let him rest until it is successfully accomplished ... but the best laid plans, that men *sometimes* make, have a habit of going astray, whether in this cause for good or evil, only the events of this night could foretell."

As the rather shifty-eyed Everest walks down the street, showcasing an evil intensity in his gaze, we react with shock as he steps off curb and almost gets mowed down by a car, his head bouncing off the lamp post behind him, as he slumps to the pavement. While citizens try their best to help him, the embarrassed Everest refuses help and stumbles off in a haze to the nearest bar.

Three young people—Charlie Kent (Loren Tindall), his fiancée Francie

Lang (Jeff Donnell) and Francie's sister Jean (Janis Carter, the tall leggy blonde who played the newspaper reporter, Pat, in the previous entry)—sit at a table in a bar/restaurant in Greenwich Village, playing gin, and observing the people around them. Jean insists on reading their fortunes with a deck of cards, but they refuse. But when the eerie, disoriented Everest enters, Jean reads his fortune from afar. The cards decree he will die within 24 hours. She reshuffles the cards and gets the same fortune a second time. When Everest exits almost as soon as he enters, Jean feels the urge to inform the handsome stranger of the fate awaiting him (even though her party screams for her to stop acting like a school girl). And with this novel pretense, the third *Whistler* begins. The formerly sinister man, now an amnesia victim, sweaty and shaky not knowing who he is, reverts to playing the benevolent character from his former *Whistler* appearances. Jean even invites him to spend the night in the apartment she shares with sister Francie (on the couch, of course).

So *The Power of the Whistler* starts off taking the track of a man attempting

Francie awakens to find her beloved pet canary dead in its cage, as sympathetic Jean and the psycho-in-an-apron "George" (Richard Dix) look on.

"George" tries to remember his past identity by going to a ballet studio, with Jean, where he traces a receipt for two dozen roses he sent to the studio, from *The Power of the Whistler*.

to retrace his steps to re-discover his own lost identity. Jean asks the man to empty his pockets to discover any clues, and the man deposits the following effects—a cigarette lighter, a doctor's prescription, an order for a birthday cake, a Canadian dollar with a license plate number penciled in, a train schedule with Woodville circled and a receipt for two dozen roses, sent to a ballet dancer. Within these unrelated clues lies the answer to the riddle. The question immediately arises—does Everest actually suffer from amnesia or is he hiding his identify and motives? Jean decides to name her strange new nameless friend George.

In suspenseful rapid-fire succession, Jean and George follow the clues and discover very little. The ballet dancer who received George's flowers does not recognize him, or so she says. And the doctor's address only leads to a used bookstore that carries a book written by a man with the doctor's name, a 50-year-old book about poison.

Of course George first appears innocent and disoriented, but once Jean brings him home for the night, the man's sinister personality emerges. Sister Francie loves her precious pet bird that she covers and wishes a good night, as a daily ritual. However, by morning time, the chirping bird, whose cage rests near the couch that George occupies, is mysteriously dead. The implications are clear. In another sequence, as Jean dresses the couch with sheets and pillows, the shadow of George appears to loom menacingly on the wall behind her. The camera quickly pans to the left to reveal a crazed George staring with his gaze lingering much too long on the unaware Jean. In other words, director Landers is telegraphing the man's evil intent to the audience, while the innocent Jean is unaware of what we just saw. As George approaches the still unaware Jean, she is startled and emits a scream, while a calm George apologizes for frightening her. That night the girls chat away in their bright bedroom. The light of the girls' bedroom is contrasted to the dark shadows that hover across the troubled face of George, echoed by a passing police siren outside and the chirping of the still-living bird. But by morning George is donning an apron and making the ladies breakfast and even washing dishes from the previous evening. He even starts the meal by saying grace. Director Landers takes care to illustrate contrasting sides of the man's character.

The question remains whether or not George is aware of his previous identity as William Everest. The Whistler provides a partial answer. "It's a bright day in the park … yet why should one man on this bench provide the sole, tumultuous exception? Does he himself realize the brash discord? What cells and what tissue in that pounding brain of yours have come back to life? Or have they?" During this narration, George sits on a park bench as a little squirrel climbs up on his lap and eats from his hand. He at first smiles, but as the camera closes in, the eyes of George bulge and nervously dart from side to side. In a simple B-movie psychological lesson, the camera reveals the inner conflicts that co-exist inside this masterfully created character. Moments later Jean meets George, still at the park bench, but now he has his hand bandaged and a few feet away rests a dead squirrel. Unlike before, George now acts suspiciously toward Jean's efforts to discover his identity, as if he were beginning to remember his past. He even makes Jean promise to keep any information uncovered quiet among the two of them.

At the same time, Francie discovers that George went to see a printer to have blank doctor prescription forms made up and immediately afterward visited an adjacent pharmacist and had a prescription filled for deadly poison. Francie's worried face and understanding

Jean and "George" walk through the park, not far from the spot where a squirrel lies dead, from *The Power of the Whistler*.

of these events reflect the audience's own concern. Then she discovers that George ordered a birthday cake, picked it up, but brought it back later to the shop to be delivered to the Hudson Mental Institution, for Warden John Crawford.

As George and Jean sit at an outdoor café, the Whistler tells us that George, when sitting on the park bench, remembered who he was, William Everest. But our narrator asks, why hasn't Everest told Jean? Of course such spooky narration only attests to flaws in the script where the audience has to be told too much plot information. But such narration only intensifies the tension. Remember, we are in B-movie territory and small plot holes are expected.

The film's final 20 minutes explode with nail-biting suspense. Jean, attracted to Everest, is unaware not just of the man's real name but also of his past life. It seems Everest was mentally insane and committed to the Hudson Mental Institution, but he somehow escaped. After his auto mishap and momentary memory loss, he now plans to murder the warden of the mental hospital by sending the poison birthday cake to his home. In the meanwhile Everest now tells Jean he remembers only one name, a Judge Nesbitt, who lives in Woodville, and they take the first train available to find the Judge. Jean wishes to phone Francie first but is unable to reach her before they depart. What Jean does not know is that Everest plans to kill the judge because he was the man who signed his commitment papers. Jean, of course, is unaware that Everest now remembers his identity and is planning a double homicide. The cinematography by L.W. O'Connell photographs the model of the train speeding to Woodville, zooming through the dark rural landscape, its engine puffing out smoke, as a thunder storm rages and lightning paints the sky and thunder crackles. Such ominous imagery only makes the viewer more apprehensive about Jean's fate. In the meanwhile Charlie and Francie work fast to prove to the police the horror that Everest is about to unleash.

Arriving in Woodville, alone on the rain-drenched train platform, Everest is now all crazy eyes and guilty expressions, while Jean is oblivious with romantic eyes and a wide smile. While Jean waits at he

Jean does not know the actual identify of the man she is attempting to help, the man who is planning two murders for revenge, from *The Power of the Whistler*.

depot, Everest goes to a borrowed car and hears a police report over the radio making him aware that a police dragnet has been created to capture "the mad man." Police have been told to shoot to kill. When Jean jumps in the car, Everest simply turns off the radio. Meanwhile the police arrive at Warden Crawford's house and save his family from the cake. So now the full focus is on capturing Everest. Crawford reveals that Everett snuck into his house, after the escape, and stole a suit of his clothes.

When a police patrol car stops Everest, he immediately tells the policemen that he is Warden Crawford and is traveling with his nurse Carol, trying to apprehend one of his former patients who escaped. He even knows that Crawford had his name written inside his breast pocket as further proof of his identity. Everett's fast thinking was clever, but such an immediate fabricated tale only makes Jean all the more wary. At this point Jean half-heartedly attempts to mouth something to the police, she at last realizing the danger she must be in. After the police leave Jean grills Everest, but the cool thinker pleads memory loss once again. But Jean notes his almost too well rehearsed story and she remains fearful.

As the police close in, Everest outsmarts the cordon and drives up to the judge's house. As Everest prepares to meet the judge, he puts his arm around Jean's shoulder, and using the other hand, brandishes a deadly knife from his pocket. Jean discovers the tag Hudson Mental Institution inside Everest's suit and screams out in fear. Everest's dialogue, delivered in total calmness, is masterful.

"This moment is set apart from time. I want to prolong it ... that wonderful throat ... that wonderful channel through which the innermost secrets of the soul find freedom to the world. Let it live, it can tell the world too much. Destroy it and its secrets are locked forever ..."

At this point Jean rushes out of the car and runs into the beautifully composed forest that surrounds the judge's house. In stark shades of blacks and grays, offset by harsh light and shadows, Jean tries to keep one step ahead of Everest as she runs and hides. Jean sneaks into the nearby barn. Everest rants about how he will spare Jean from much of life's torment ... he will keep her forever young ... time and life are the enemy and Everest is the friend who can save her from reality. In other words, the man is totally bonkers. Jean manages to climb up to the upper loft in the barn to fend off the madman. Once again O'Connell's photography is masterful with low angle shadowy shots of the frightened Jean wielding a pitchfork juxtaposed to a high angle shot of Everest climbing up the wooden steps as light and shadow play on his face, flashing an unnerving smile as he ascends. Jean flings the pitchfork into her pursuer's chest, killing him.

The final sequence shows the lumbering shadow of the Whistler walking down a street. Once again the film ends with his narration. "In a city full of strange adventures, this has been one of the most amazing. Protected by the resilience of youth, Jean Lang will carry no scars on her soul from her encounter with William Everest. And as time passes even the nightmare memory will not disturb her innocent sleep. She will marry in time a man destined for her and live long and happily in the fullness of her years. I know, for I am the Whistler."

This third entry, *The Power of the Whistler*, contains much strength and few flaws, making it ultimately a very worthy entry. L.L. O'Connell's intense cinematography brings back the film noir look missing from the second entry. The suspenseful final 20-minutes succeeds mostly because of his creative photography. Richard Dix's performance plays off against the honesty and sincerity of the first two *Whistler* performances, at first making his William Everest a mirror image of his earlier character roles. But his clever use of a grimace, an intense stare, rolling eyeballs and madman's face make his transition from small time criminal to full-blown psychopath quite effective. Janis Carter, who plays Jean Lang, graduated from a supporting reporter's role in the previous entry and does a fine job here. Beautiful in a sisterly rather than a sensual way, Jean is required to play innocence because the audience needs to come to understand Everest's evil before she does. That's the entire point. Jean is a young innocent who is unaware of the dark underbelly that life sometimes offers and she plays her innocence well. Yes, the plot depends a tad too much on narration (of course this is the *Whistler* series and his psychological overseeing is what drives the series) and once again the plot seems a little rushed and sometimes silly. But, all in all, *The Power of the Whistler* is an effective B-production combining elements of the follow-the-clues mystery genre, as we watch a young

girl fall into the clutches of a madman. And Lew Landers' direction is crisp and does a good job conveying both the calm innocence and over-the-top ravings of a psycho killer as the economic plot unfolds.

With the fourth *Whistler* entry, William Castle returned to the fold by both directing and co-writing (along with Wilfred H. Petitt) 1945's *Voice of the Whistler*, featuring mesmerizing cinematography by George Meehan. Earlier entries all occurred among urban settings, with the typical film noir flourishes that only dark city streets could provide. But *Voice of the Whistler* occurs equally divided between a small town American burgh and a ghostly seaside lighthouse. And wisely, the series expands its visual tableau to produce an entry that feels different, even though star Richard Dix returns, but he plays a slightly different type of role. For me, four pictures into the series, *Voice of the Whistler* feels revitalized and fresh.

The theme of loneliness and isolation comes front and center, and the theme is explored through two of the main characters, John Sinclair/John Carter (Richard Dix) and Joan Martin/Joan Sinclair (Lynn Merrick). The movie opens as the silhouette of the Whistler appears overtop the rocks on the shore near a misty, spooky lighthouse. We are told that a mysterious woman lives alone in a long abandoned lighthouse and never leaves its premises, and the movie provides the story how she came to live such an isolated life. "Hers is the story of loneliness and greed."

In a rather obvious tribute, *Voice of the Whistler* begins with a low-rent homage to *Citizen Kane*, as its similar industrialist hero, John Sinclair, rises to the top of the world via a series of movie newsreel snippets. But the years have taken their toll on the aging Golden Boy, as he stands before his corporate board, sweating and weak, suffering from a serious heart ailment that may claim his life. Even with all his success, it is clear that Sinclair is lonely at the top and has absolutely no close friends or surviving relatives. At his home alone Sinclair sits down to a game of chess, as the narration of the Whistler begins.

"Suspicion and distrust in his fellow man have driven John Sinclair to solitude. There has been no time for love or companionship in his ruthless drive for power and riches. Even over his chess game he cannot relax. For it is through the medium of these ivory pawns that he plans the strategy to expand his enormous holdings. But without realizing it, he has already strained body and mind beyond endurance." At this point Sinclair collapses to the floor and awakens in his bed, under a doctor's care. The doctor tells Sinclair's servant that another of these attacks might be fatal and the doctor orders an immediate vacation and long rest.

Stopping off at a small town dock to catch the ship for his ocean voyage, Sinclair suffers an attack and is rescued by taxicab driver Ernie Sparrow (Rhys Williams), who cares for him. The Brit assures Sinclair that he is among friends here. Sparrow was a professional

Industrialist Sinclair loves to play chess, the game becoming a metaphor for cleverness and deception, from *Voice of the Whistler*.

lightweight boxing champion with fame and fortune, but the strain of fame only led to problems (who were true friends and who were the hangers-on?), so he gave it all up and came to live in this small American town, where literally everyone knows him simply as their neighbor. He was lonely because he never trusted anyone, for he never had time to get to know people. Now Sparrow is happy because he has true friends. Sparrow advises Sinclair to do the same, to walk away from the strain of wealth and fame for the anonymous world of contentment and fellowship. Sparrow tells Sinclair he has to learn to trust people again.

Sparrow drops Sinclair off at the local medical clinic where he meets Dr. Fred Graham (James Cardwell) and nurse Joan Martin. Sinclair uses the name "Carter" to avoid recognition and Carter delivers flowers to the beautiful nurse, a gift from Sparrow. Carter at first reluctantly sees the elder Dr. Rose who tells Carter that his lab reports are not favorable. The doctor advises him to go up the coast of Maine, breathe in the sea air, get a job and make friends. "Loneliness is a disease that can destroy a man's mind." The implication is that a man can die from simply having a lack of friends.

Meanwhile, Fred Graham is engaged to Nurse Martin and wants to elope next weekend. However, the pragmatic Joan says she won't chain their lives to an environment like this. She insisted earlier, before agreeing to marry him, that Fred must have his own practice established, with some money saved to purchase a home.

Carter and Sparrow talk about the doctor's advice to spend six months at the sea coast of Maine "for health and happiness." Sparrow, thinking that Carter needs money to finance the extended trip, is shocked when Carter tells him he has plenty of money. But he asks his friend to put his cab in storage for six months and join him. Sparrow, giggling, readily accepts. Before leaving, Carter wants to have lunch with Joan Martin. Carter makes her a business proposal, asking her to marry him. For his few remaining months of life, he will have a lifetime of passion to share with Joan, and in return, his entire fortune will go to her upon his death. Later, now knowing that John Carter is John Sinclair, Joan meets with fiancé Fred. Fred states he will have his own practice in a little while and kisses Joan, but Joan delivers the hard, cold facts. She informs Fred that she intends to marry Sinclair and that this will give them everything they ever wanted. Joan wants Fred's approval. Confused, Fred lashes out at Joan telling her to admit the truth, that she never cared for him, that she is doing this because she is selfish. "You are not satisfied to wait and to work hard like any normal, decent woman would do. I do not think you are being dishonest, I think you're rotten!"

Joan responds, "This is my chance. For four years I waited for you! Being in love with someone I never see. I'm human! Oh Fred I do love you, I always will. I've given you the chance to get ahead and you failed. Now I'm going to do it my way. I believe in you, but you are soft. You've been afraid. You're always letting other people push you down. Fred, try to understand."

Smirking, Fred rises and calls Joan "Mrs. Sinclair," thanking her for everything, and leaves.

In this low-rent film noir world of moral ambivalence, the sizzling Joan Martin can seem sincere and loving, but Fred is correct when he accuses her of being rotten, of not working toward their mutual goal through decent means. And

Set mainly amid the gloomy lighthouse, we see Ernie Sparrow (Rhys Williams) playing chess, with Joan (Lynn Merrick) and Sinclair (Richard Dix) front and center, from *Voice of the Whistler*.

Laughter... a prelude to murder!

Sinclair, Sparrow and Joan in happier times, having just met in generic small-town America, from *Voice of the Whistler*.

those final lines Joan delivers to Fred cut deeply. It is only too clear that greed is the motivation behind her actions. And while she may not be evil, she is most definitely not the innocent young nurse that the audience originally perceived.

Time passes and John Sinclair converts an abandoned lighthouse into a beach house for the trio, and Sinclair spends most of his days playing chess (symbolic of his cleverness and well-plotted deception). However, the cozy life has improved Sinclair's health and his death no longer seems imminent, even though six months have passed. And by this time Sinclair admits to falling in love with his business-arranged wife. Sparrow advises Sinclair to come clean, apologize to her for being alive for so long and tell Joan that she is the reason he has not died. But as the dripping beauty emerges from the seaside beach, she seems cold, aloof and unhappy. That night Sinclair wants to have an intimate walk down the beach with Joan, when Joan reveals she is leaving him. Citing the total isolation of living alone without going anywhere or having any friends visit is too great a burden. Joan says she hates it here. When Sinclair mentions the bargain they made, Joan rants that she kept her end of the bargain, but John has not kept his (meaning he has not died within six months as expected). Sinclair accuses her of missing her young doctor friend, but she admits that was true at first, but now that relationship is over. Joan states it's just this lonely place. To demonstrate his love for Joan, Sinclair agrees to sell the lighthouse and travel to all the places she wanted to go. But just at this point when Sinclair and Joan are cementing their relationship, Fred Graham just happens to appear at the lighthouse for a visit. Joan is visibly excited to see her old fiancé. Of course, although he wears a glad smile, Sinclair feels threatened.

When Joan tells Fred that Sinclair has a passion for playing chess, and that he has been teaching her how to play, Fred puts his cards on the table. "Joan, when you play chess with him, don't you get a feeling of being trapped? Just a feeling I got … that you are not really happy being here." Fred says, "I will make you see things my way." At this point Sinclair arrives and welcomes Fred with open arms. It is an awkward moment, but Sinclair feels he has totally won Joan over to his way of thinking, so Fred is no longer a threat. However, while Fred and Joan talk on the beach later that evening, lounging on a large rock, Joan tells Fred that she stayed with John for six months shut away from the world and now she intends to collect for every minute of that time. She tells Fred to be patient, that she really wants to be with him, but she needs time. Fred says that Joan was right about how he was soft and let people push him around. He will now do things his way. And a new sense of ruthlessness emerges from Fred that we never observed before. From the window Sinclair watches as Fred and Joan embrace and kiss passionately.

Using a chess playing philosophy, Sinclair creates a scenario in which he could murder Fred and get away with the perfect crime. And he playfully presents the plan to Fred. It involves Sinclair telling Sparrow that he caught Fred sleepwalking and roaming near the huge lighthouse solarium windows. Eventually Sinclair would murder Fred and throw his body out the solarium window, and the rocks and tide would do the rest. In Sinclair's scenario, a sleepwalker meets an accidental death. "In chess that's known as checkmate!" Of course Sinclair was planting an idea in Fred's brain, expecting his rival in love to fall for his bait. As the Whistler explains, "What did he mean by that game of chess? Is he planning to kill you or only trying to frighten you? You better leave here before it is too late. You've lost Joan already or is there something you can do about it?"

It is Fred who tells Sparrow that John has been sleepwalking and asks Sparrow to go out and buy locks for the windows. Sparrow states it is Sunday, stores are closed, but Fred says Monday will work out just as well. Fred asks Sparrow to keep his mouth shut. Next, Fred is in town buying a powdered sedative and in the next sequence, back at the lighthouse, Fred passes a cup of coffee to Sinclair, the Whistler letting us know that the drink contains the sedative. Sinclair sniffs the coffee but does not drink it, but Joan enters with a very guilty expression.

Sinclair passes his coffee to Joan, since her own coffee is now cold.

Sinclair, the chess-playing strategist, is awaiting an appearance from Fred in his bedroom at 4 a.m. Sinclair is waiting for Fred in the shadows, but where? Cinematographer George Meehan produces some of his moodiest camerawork in this sequence. The sequence begins as the darkness surrounding an alarm clock lifts, revealing the early hour. A low-angle shot watches as Fred climbs the spiral staircase cloaked in shadows. Fred enters John's bedroom, his face bathed in darkness. As he reaches for his metal poker, the tool slips and makes a noise. A close-up on Fred's face reveals wide terrified eyes, greasy hair, beads of sweat and a madly determined expression. After beating the supposed victim beneath the covers four hard blows, his facial expression erupting in satisfaction with each blow, he stops, flips the covers back and discovers that Sinclair is not in the bed. The medium shot is atmospherically framed. Fred stands in the shadows, only the metal rod in his hand reflecting light. The covers on the bed are bathed in a bright light, apparently from the bedroom window. The rays of sunlight paint the wallpaper behind Fred at an angle making Fred the center of focus. By this time Fred sweats profusely, his hair mussed and falling in strings upon his face. He mutters, "Where are you; I know you are here," realizing that Sinclair has cleverly lured him here. The camera pans left and right, becoming Fred's paranoid eyes, searching in the shadows for Sinclair. Suddenly Sinclair emerges from the corner blackness and, armed with his own metal rod, strikes with a crushing blow to Fred's skull. So it seems that the clever Sinclair has out-foxed Fred. But Sinclair must throw Fred's body to the rocks below so the coroner cannot tell he was bludgeoned to death before he fell. However the windows are nailed shut (good friend Sparrow would not be able to get to the store until Monday, so he nailed all the windows shut to protect his friend). Sinclair has only one choice, to carry Fred's corpse down to the rocks and lay him there. Sinclair's expressions are caught in close up, half of his face disappearing into shadows, his eyes bulging and mind deep in thought. Sweat is dripping down his face.

Down on the rocky beach, Sparrow catches Sinclair in the act of smashing the corpse with a large rock. Sparrow nailed the windows shut, so he knows that Sinclair is lying when he tells his friend that Fred fell from the lighthouse. Returning to the house, Sinclair finds Joan waiting and she accuses him of murdering Fred, for she saw him carrying the corpse downstairs. Joan rushes out to call the police. Sparrow comforts his good friend by telling him it's too late now, he'll just have to face the consequences.

As the moody night-lit shot of the lighthouse returns, the shadow of the Whistler returns to deliver his end-of-picture narration. "... The jury did not believe John's story and he paid the extreme penalty for the murder of Fred Graham. Joan inherited the Sinclair millions and ... the life of luxury she had always craved ... but constantly haunting her was the tragedy that cost the lives of the man she loved and the man she married. ... There was no escape from the past. She came back at last to live out a life of torment in the solitude and desolation of the lighthouse. I know because—I am the Whistler."

Voice of the Whistler, four deep in the series of eight, demonstrates why this little B-programmer series shines. We have another effective, though different, performance from star Richard Dix. We have a low-budget homage alluding to one of the greatest movies of all time, *Citizen Kane*. We have a triangle of two men loving one woman, where all three characters evolve and become someone different than who we first imagined each to be. Joan is a beautiful young nurse who desires an affluent life, yet we never visualized her as the rotten, selfish character that Fred knows her to be. And after Joan calls Fred soft and too easily manipulated, Fred mistakenly throws his morals out to sea when he returns to the lighthouse to take the love of his life back, at any cost. The fact that Fred would murder for the woman he called a rotten person only attests to the old adage about love being blind. Even Sinclair, the clever industrialist, succumbs to his baser instincts and plots to murder his wife's lover so he could have her all to himself. In the best image of the femme fatale, the audience realizes that, besides her sizzling body, Joan has little to offer the two men in her life, except tons of trouble. We know that she is not worth the effort, but the blinded-by-love halfwits do not realize their weaknesses until it is too late for either of them. The only character that wins, for a while, is Joan, who inherits Sinclair's fortune. But her guilt forces her back to a life of isolation at the lighthouse. Not even Joan can escape her morals. And the entire taut hour-long B-movie is drenched in shadowy photography and an alluring mystery that occurs for the most part in a horrific lighthouse bathed by moonlight. B-movies don't get much better.

The fifth entry in the *Whistler* series, 1946's *Mysterious Intruder* (the first to eliminate a Whistler association in the title), again features director William Castle and star Richard Dix,

this entry formulated around a story and screenplay written by Eric Taylor with cinematography by Philip Tannura. In this outing the movie's goals are a tad less ambitious, with a return to a fully urban environment and more claustrophobic (i.e. low-budget) set pieces. Richard Dix plays Don Gale, a P.I. teetering on the brink of corruption, the series attempting to play to the newly successful sub-genre of detective/mystery movies that hit it big in the 1940s. However, *Mysterious Intruder* is no *The Big Sleep* or *The Maltese Falcon*. But it is a rather ambitious little B-programmer that again focuses on moral conflict and how everyone pays for the bad decisions made in life.

As the shadow of the Whistler walks from almost complete darkness to street-lit nighttime, his shadow is passed by the hustling shadow of elderly shopkeeper, Edward Stillwell. "It is Edward Stillwell who walks alone. He is a kindly, unimportant little man, the type you pass on the street but do not notice. Tonight, however, something will happen to him that changes everything … something to make his life important, exciting and dangerous."

Stillwell (Paul E. Burns), a humble immigrant shop owner, wants to hire slick private detective Don Gale (Richard Dix) to find a young woman from the neighborhood, Elora Lund (Pamela Blake), who has been missing for seven years (since she was 14). When Stillwell politely refuses to reveal his reasons for wanting to find the girl, Gale gets huffy and loud, trying to size up the man and size up the amount of money he has to offer. Philip Tannura's camerawork attracts immediate attention as the shadows of the office cover Stillwell's face in the foreground as the harshly and brightly lit Gale, more animated, turns in his chair, rises and walks across the back of his office, a huge window showcasing a suspension bridge outside. Later the frame changes with Stillwell sitting in a chair in the background brightly lit while Gale lounges on his sofa, chewing on a cigar, his face buried half in darkness. This sequence is basically showing talking heads and faces with the purpose of establishing complex background information and the arrogant persona of Gale. The gritty cinematography maintains our attention. Don Gale's character is clearly revealed when he announces that finding the woman will take lots of money. When Stillwell proclaims confidently that he has $100, Gale only smirks, laughs and bellows annoyingly, "Can't you dig a little deeper? Can't you raise a little money?" This is when Stillwell reveals that if the P.I. finds Elora, she will have a small fortune to pay him anything he requires. But Stillwell remains mum on the details, which both intrigues and angers Gale. Gale speaks of the mutual trust that must exist between client and detective, but the audience easily realizes that Gale is a man not to be trusted.

In one of the movie's standout sequences, three nights later, after Stillwell

Imposter Freda Hanson (Helen Mowery) gets roughed up by private investigator Don Gale (Richard Dix). Gale is more interested in money than helping his clients.

In a publicity shot, Pontos (Mike Mazurki) stands by his bed, moments before he is shot to death, with Gale standing in the shadowy background.

reveals to Gale that he placed an ad in the local paper to find Elora Lund, a beautiful blonde claiming to be Lund appears at Stillwell's shop, after closing time. Also lingering outside, standing in the shadows, is the looming figure of huge Harry Pontos (Mike Mazurki), who watches the woman from a distance. Stillwell and Lund have an intimate conversation and Stillwell reveals that Elora's mother sold him family heirlooms (from Sweden) for some needed ready cash. Stillwell kept all these heirlooms thinking, when Mrs. Lund got on her feet again, she would buy them back. Stillwell does not explain but hands the woman a newspaper article that explains that one of these heirlooms will make her a rich woman. Stillwell excuses himself to find Gale and let him in on the news, but after the old man exits, Pontos enters the shop and begins to root around. The shop—now lit in shades of gray, white and black, with dank shadows rendering it a scary place—becomes more ominous with the appearance of the huge intruder. As Pontos slowly climbs down a narrow cellar staircase, his shadow lumbering behind appears gigantic. However, when Stillwell returns, Pontos hides in the shadows. Pontos emerges from the shadows, smiling, and calmly puts his huge hands around the shopkeeper's throat, brandishing a sharp knife and stabbing the kindly man fatally. Pontos, still smiling, approaches the terrified blonde with the knife extended toward her. Not harming the blonde, he grabs her and forces her back into a side room.

Of course it is Gale who finds Stillwell dead and gets interviewed by reporters, telling them, surprisingly, that the woman who claimed to be Elora Lund was an imposter. Of course, how does he know this information?

Clearing matters up, Gale goes to a hotel room, knocks on the door, and the woman who pretended to be Elora Lund answers, her personality and diction now much less innocent and refined than the ruse she created for Stillwell. The blonde's name is Freda Hanson (Helen Mowery), and she's a photographic mod-el who does side work for the private detective. When the smiling Gale asks if she killed Stillwell, she slaps him. Gale claims to have saved her life by telling the reporters that she was not the actual Elora Lund, allowing ruthless Pontos to release her when he hears the facts over the radio. But she is very upset at Gale for putting her in that dangerous predicament. Gale hired her to find out the reason why Stillwell wanted to find Elora Lund. Freda's hotel manager, a cold and soft-spoken man named Summers (Regis Toomey), knocks on the door interrupting the arguing couple to demand that Gale leave, that he is disturbing the other guests.

With Freda's help, Gale and she drive to the house where Pontos held her

Don Gale and Freda Hanson outside the Pontos house, with Gale about to learn of the deceptive nature of his hired assistant.

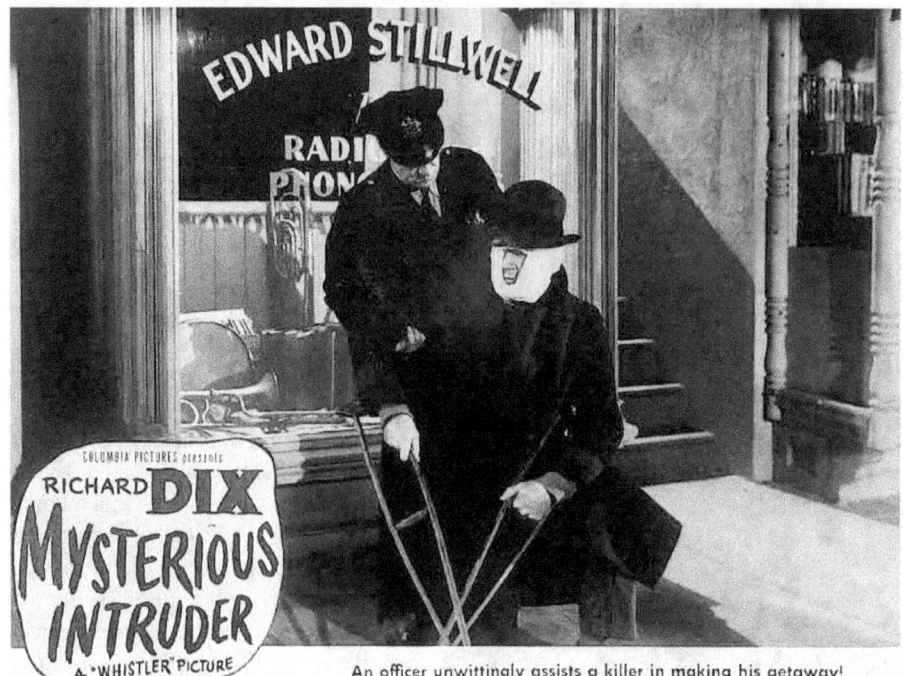

An officer unwittingly assists a killer in making his getaway!

Tricky Don Gale, donning a radical disguise, evades the police and is able to sneak into the store adjacent to Stillwell's.

captive before releasing her. Gale enters the house while Freda waits in the car, and he finds the drunk and unconscious Pontos on the floor next to his bed, a bottle in hand. At the same time two cops arrive, Taggart (Barton MacLane) and Burns (Charles Lane), guns blasting, and they kill Pontos. Gale escapes outside the back window but loses a shoe, which the police find and us to identify Gale later. Philip Tannura's photography makes this sequence another delight, as shadows of trees and Gale himself drape the front of the Pontos house. Gale sneaks through the kitchen and hallways, at one point kicking a bottle left in the hall that startles the audience. The bedroom is another wonderfully lit focus of darkness and shadows. Even the sequence where Gale finds Pontos, which consists of a quick high angle shot from over Gale's shoulder looking down at the sleeping Pontos, is startling. The quick cuts between the two cops entering from the front and Gale escaping from the rear elicits tension. Gale jumps in the car and rejoins Freda, and in a sustained long glance, Gale stares at the odometer and then looks at Freda. Something unstated is wrong.

Concurrently, the actual Elora Lund, recovering from an auto accident at a local sanatorium, reads a newspaper article about Stillwell's death and the Elora Lund impersonator. The police intervene and the real Lund agrees to cooperate with them. The police suspect that Gale sent the imposter to grill Stillwell before he was killed, and they want Lund to speak with Gale, to get to the bottom of this sordid case. The police also want Gale to reveal to them the name of the girl he hired as impersonator, but Gale keeps quiet about Freda. When Gale goes to Freda's apartment, letting her know that he knows she drove 1/10 of a mile to phone the police about Pontos, suspecting they would arrive with guns blazing and most likely shoot Gale dead as well. Gale knows that Freda planned to double-cross him for Stillwell's money and she needed to get him out of the way so Pontos (the man she hired and worked with) and her would get the $200,000 mentioned in Stillwell's newspaper clipping. It seems that the Swedish Nightingale, singer Jenny Lind, recorded two wax recordings six months before she died. Each wax cylinder is worth $100,000. And Elora's mother owned these wax recordings, which she sold to Stillwell.

The real Elora Lund comes to Gale's office and reads the Jenny Lind newspaper article. She tells Gale that she remembers the wax records that Lind made for her grandfather, but Gale tells her she has no proof that these recordings are hers. But Gale says, for a 25% cut (citing the risks he will be taking), he will capture Stillwell's murderer and recover the wax recordings for her. Lund is concerned about Gale's illegal methods, but the slyly smiling Gale tells her turning a murderer over to the police is not illegal, implying the rest is best left unsaid.

In the film's rapid-fire and complex climax, the body of Freda is found dead,

Two men... two guns... shoot it out in the shadows!

The climactic gun fight in the cellar does not end well for Don Gale.

strangled and hanging in the closet. The hotel manager, Mr. Summers, found the body and tried to revive her, but he was six hours too late. He seems apologetic for moving the corpse, but the police understand. Since Don Gale has been seen in Freda's company, the police issue a warrant for his arrest.

Gale's secretary finds Gale half-loaded in a bar and warns him. But in a cold and ruthless conversation, Gale tells Joan that he plans to recover the wax recordings and then head for the border, apparently robbing Elora Lund of her rightful property. It seems that Mr. Brown, who owns the store adjacent to Stillwell's shop, was Stillwell's best friend and Gale suspects that the wax recordings might be hidden in the cellar of Brown's shop. So, Gale sneaks into the building wearing a disguise. The police are already on the scene waiting for him. But Gale has already gained access to Brown's store, but Mr. Brown lies murdered on the floor. In the cellar below, hotel manager Mr. Summers and his accomplice are rummaging through stored junk, trying to find the recordings. Gale observes silently from the shadows above, allowing the two men below to do all the work. Almost ready to give up, the men find a box with the recordings hidden in a large bass drum. Gale, who already drew a pistol from his suit pocket, now enters the scene. Gale knows that Summers was working with Freda and Pontos, but of course they are both dead. So when Summers offers to cut Gale in on the deal, Gale is too smart to be Summer's next victim and former partner. In the half-darkness, a shuffle ensues and a bullet wounds Gale. But he shoots Summers, who is holding the box with the wax cylinders. Surprisingly, running upstairs, Gale calls the police and tells them to come to Brown's shop, that he has everything wrapped up. But as he starts to walk back down the stairs, he thinks the second gunman is waiting for him, so Gale fires a shot. In actuality, two cops are below and they open fire on the unsuspecting Gale killing him. Ironically, a stray bullet shoots through the wooden box shattering the wax recordings. Now no one will benefit from Mr. Stillwell's decades old good deed.

"So after long years of balancing precariously on the borderline of the

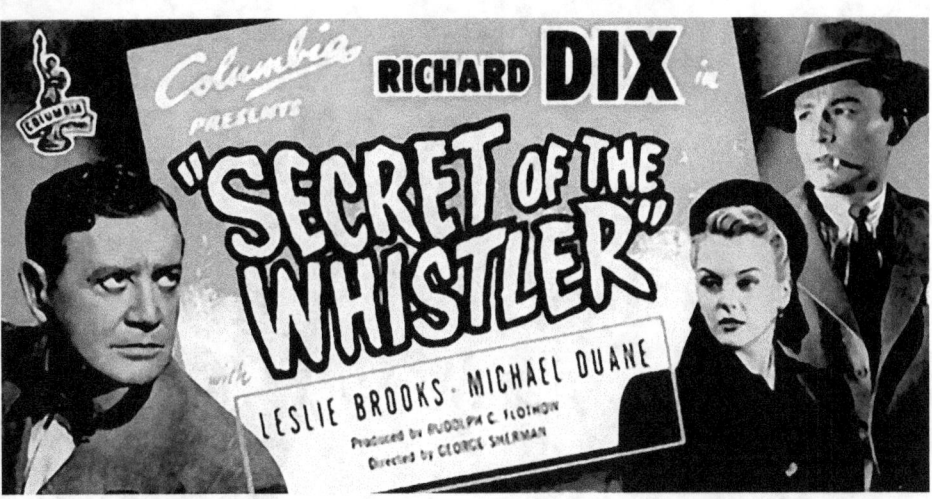

law, Don Gale was trying at the end to do the right thing, but he made one fatal mistake … Taggart and Burns will never know that Gale's shots were not meant for them."

One of the strengths of this low-budget B-series is the original and often complex story that must unravel in a mere hour of running time. Sometimes the writers have to cheat and take short cuts, and sometimes not all the pieces of the puzzle fit together perfectly, but the plots are always different and manage to engage the audience. The one common aspect, besides the always-pleasurable appearance of Richard Dix (even though he's a little pudgy, rather mature for a leading man and not ruggedly handsome), is the psychological undertone of each story. The plot always manages to illuminate the demons lurking inside the mind of whatever character Dix plays in that particular movie. Avoiding simple labels of good and evil, the complexities of internal character struggles and moral choices hang heavily in each film. Most of his characters appear to be flawed, but even when considering their teetering moral frailty, the characters are usually likable. Perhaps we see our own lives in these little moral fables that cut like a knife.

The next *Whistler* entry, 1946's *The Secret of the Whistler*, while still entertaining, is generally one of the weaker entries ignoring those qualities that made the series such a success. Perhaps replacing director William Castle with George Sherman might be at the root of the problem. We might also finger-point the screenplay written by Raymond L. Schrock, which replaces the series' moonlight-lit cityscape, substituting the ethnic-based and poor urban underbelly with the affluent, bright mansions of the upper-crust society. Shadowy cinematography is replaced with piercing shafts of sunlight. The cinematography by Allen Siegler is quite competent, but there's little sense of the film noir environment to be observed in his camerawork. Of course the challenge of any B-series is to keep things fresh and evolving, so perhaps this transformation from shades of gray to shades of white was deliberate. However, the dark shades of moral ambiguity are still front and center in the screenplay. And we have Richard Dix back with another variation of his morally bankrupt weasel character, which has apparently replaced his gentler and more sympathetic earlier performances in the series.

Still walking in the cloak of night, the Whistler delivers his brief opening monologue: "And tonight, in this obscure section of a large city, we find a woman shopping for an unusual item." The woman, middle aged and dressed in black, with a black net over her face, is at the Curtis Monument Company picking out her own tombstone and inscription (selecting the most expensive model, crafted in marble). The only thing she cannot supply is the exact date of her death, but from her morbid dress and personality, the audience realizes she does not have long to wait. Her name is Edith Marie Harrison (Mary Currier).

Cut to a glitzy party, with scores of fashionable people milling about, hosted by Ralph Harrison (Richard Dix), the oddball, unsuccessful artist and husband of the formerly viewed Edith Harrison.

Ralph is smitten when artist model Kay Morrell (Leslie Brooks), a sizzling hot blonde wearing a risqué bare-shoulder black gown, enters as guest of Ralph's friend, Jim Calhoun (Michael Duane), also an artist. Ralph dutifully attends to his guests. The slightly puffy and over-the-hill Ralph notices Kay's voluptuous figure from the rear, all her curves on display, standing unattended. Ralph eyeballs her beauty for a tad too long and asks her for a dance, flirting at every opportunity. Ralph is called to the phone and told his wife has suffered another heart attack, a serious one, and he rushes home after telling his guests to carry on. However, Ralph seems more upset over leaving Kay than worrying about his wife. But upon his exiting, all his party guests give little asides such as, "Who cares. No one is going to miss him." It is apparent that Ralph, a former fairgrounds sketch artist, has now evolved into the world of high art, and everyone knows he lacks talent and that his wealthy wife bankrolls his passions. To his peers, Ralph is a joke and people are willing to take advantage of his generosity. However Kay states sympathetically, "I don't see why everybody picks on him. I think he's rather nice." When Kay asks why people attend his party, another attractive young girl states that someone's got to drink his liquor and eat his food. When party guest and reporter Joe Conroy (Ray Walker) sees one of Ralph's paintings, *Autumn Symphony*, he almost breaks out in laughter asking his date does he sell these things? She breaks out laughing and says no, his wife gives him all the money he needs.

Returning home the family doctor tells Ralph that his wife has only weeks to a few months to live. With her specific heart condition, the doctor can do little except keep her comfortable. But Ralph returns to his now vacant art studio/apartment to find Kay's compact. His *buddy* Jim is painting the swimsuit model down the hall and Ralph asks if he can use Kay as his model when Jim is finished with her. After Ralph leaves, Jim asks Kay why she agreed to work with him. "I have to earn a living, don't I? Besides you said yourself he pays double the scale." Jim admits to being jealous, that he saw how Ralph looked at her last night at the party. But Kay caresses Jim and says, "Don't worry darling, he's just a pigeon to me."

Ralph starts posing Kay in exotic costumes to paint her, but Kay complains Ralph never finishes any portrait of her. Taking her out to lunch, Ralph confides in her, telling the young beauty about his sick wife, stating he needs Kay as a friend, someone to confide in, to dine with and to simply allow him to de-stress. Kay and Ralph do the town frequently, she always purring and smiling, perhaps remembering that when Edith dies that Ralph will inherit her fortune. And

Ralph tells Kay, if he were free, he would ask her to marry him. But Kay reminds Ralph he is not free! In the meantime Edith's doctor has brought aboard a new heart specialist to treat Edith and, almost overnight, Edith starts to improve, much to Ralph's chagrin.

It's time for the Whistler's interjections to punctuate Ralph's deep thoughts as he sits and smokes in a living room chair. As the Whistler's shadow looms over and behind Ralph, that distinct voice mutters, "You are quite concerned, aren't you Ralph. If Dr. Gunther can make Edith well again, it will spoil all your plans. You know you are only waiting and hoping for her to die, so you will be free to marry Kay!" Kay visits Jim and tells him the little job with Ralph might turn into a full fledge career, but not to worry, that little Kay won't burn the bridges with her old friends, just in the event that the "pigeon" flies away.

Edith Harrison has now improved, secretly up and about, going out for short trips. She no longer will need a home care nurse. And, of course, since all this has been a surprise to everyone except the doctor, Edith decides to visit Ralph at his studio apartment, asking the janitor to admit her but not to tell Ralph, that she wants to surprise him. Ralph and Kay return from lunch, unaware that Edith is listening from above. Kay is getting frustrated with Ralph's lack of artistic productivity and speaks of quitting him, but Ralph lays on how much he loves her, Edith's face sinking as she hears Ralph plead that he could not go on without Kay. Ralph returns home to find Edith writing a journal entry expressing her emotional pain knowing her husband loves another, younger woman. Edith admits where she was and what she heard and how Ralph is a total hypocrite for lying to her about his new lover. Edith accuses Ralph of hoping she would die so he would be free to marry a younger woman. She tells Ralph he will never get another penny out of her, but that he can keep his art studio apartment until he gets a place of his own. Edith then kicks him out.

In the movie's only sinister sequence, we find Ralph, in the middle of the night, sneaking back into Edith's house, creeping silently through the shadows that cover parts of his face and head. Going up to his wife's bedroom, he stares at her

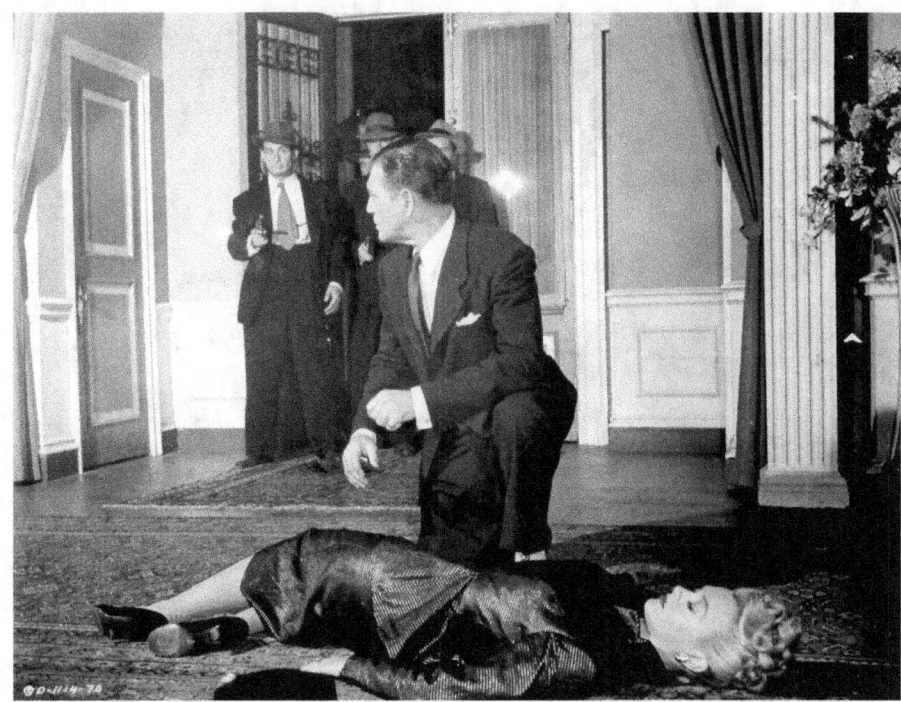

The police close in on Ralph (Richard Dix) as he bends over the corpse of his wife Kay (Leslie Brooks), from *Secret of the Whistler*.

sleeping form, takes one of her medicine bottles, and, with his back to the camera, poisons her medicine, returning the bottle to her nightstand. As Ralph creeps out of the room, Edith opens her eyes, perhaps aware of what just transpired. However, in the next sequence the servant finds Edith lying dead, next to her bed.

The Whistler makes his return appearance to comment on the proceedings. "You aren't getting unnerved, are you Ralph? Setting the stage was comparatively easy, but what now, has your wife taken the medicine, did the doctor believe she died from natural causes? It's the uncertainty of not knowing that is getting you down. Too bad you can't phone your home. There's nothing you can do but wait!" But when Ralph is summoned back to his home, he is told that his wife is dead, and asking for some time alone, he tries to retrieve her medicine bottles but they are gone.

The Whistler's shadow passes and informs us that three months have now passed since Edith's body was cremated, but that the finger of suspicion still points to Ralph. Ralph has since married Kay and brings her home to live in their totally remodeled home. But Kay is suspicious when she learns that Ralph had Edith cremated when she paid for a large burial monument (where, of course, it is implied that the body could be exhumed and examined, but *not* her ashes). Kay pokes around and finds Edith's journal, the final entry telling of Ralph's nocturnal visit to her room, he believing falsely that she was asleep, and her suspicion that Ralph poisoned her medicine. Kay uses scissors to remove that final entry. The house servant Laura (Claire Du Brey) tells Kay that the only reason she remains is to find evidence to incriminate Ralph for the death of Edith. Even Kay tells her friend Jim that she believes Ralph is a murderer. Kay brings Jim the now discovered final bottle of medicine to have its contents analyzed by his reporter pal Joe Conroy. The Whistler's narration returns, this time delivered on a tight close-up of Ralph's sweating, nervous face, citing his fear that Edith wrote something incriminating in her journal.

That night Ralph feels relieved and relaxed and wants to do the town with Kay, but Kay complains of a headache. Joe Conroy phones to inform Kay that Edith's medicine was indeed poisoned and that the police will arrive shortly. When Ralph announces he will go out on his own, Kay says she is feeling much better and just needs time to powder her nose. Ralph asks for a quick kiss, and when his wife approaches, the expression on his face changes, as his hands clutch

her throat and he calmly chokes his wife to death. "Too bad you are such a liar and a cheat. I heard you talking on the phone." Ralph's eyes are maniacal, and when the police arrive, he rushes up the stairs and is shot, but not seriously, but Kay, dead, holds the missing diary page, which implicates guilty Ralph. At the very end the camera pans and we see the gloating, satisfied face of the loyal servant as the strangely *silent* shadow of the Whistler passes as "The End" appears.

The Secret of the Whistler becomes so frustrating in ignoring many of the aspects of the series that make it memorable. Gone is the noir nighttime photography with its wealth of contrasting shadows. Gone is the sympathy we typically hold for the flawed character that Richard Dix portrays. Director Sherman added one brief sequence where Ralph's party guests mock their host and make fun of his art, but even this does not elicit sympathy when the man knowingly wishes his invalid wife would die sooner than later so he can marry his artist model girlfriend (who also sees him as her meal ticket and little more). All the major characters are obnoxious, including "friends" Jim Calhoun and newspaper hack Joe Conroy. Even wife Edith, sympathetic only because of her heart condition, always seems to come off as harsh and judgmental. This *Whistler* features one of the most obnoxious assortment of unlikable characters featured in the series and ultimately seems half-baked and unsatisfying. Even the ending comes to a crashing conclusion, and the unexpected strangulation of Kay seems more cruel than satisfying. For me this entry was the first misstep in the series. Still, the movie holds interest and Richard Dix's performance is credibly crafted.

The second to last *Whistler* entry happens to be the final entry for star Richard Dix, who retired after the completion of the movie. Two years after his retirement he suffered a fatal heart attack at age 56, culminating a movie career that started with his first role in 1917. In 1930 Dix was nominated for a Best Actor Academy Award for his starring role in the Western classic *Cimarron*. But it wasn't until his villainous role in 1943's *The Ghost Ship*, perhaps the least satisfying of the seven classic Val Lewton-produced horror-suspense thrillers, that genre fans became aware of the now aging actor. The *Whistler* movies were the only films that Richard Dix appeared in from 1944 onward. Even though these were Columbia programmers, Richard Dix received above-the-credit billing for all six appearances and created some fine characterizations of morally challenged individuals. It proved to be a dandy way to end a journeyman career.

Unfortunately, 1947's *The Thirteenth Hour* was perhaps the worst of the entire series, even a step down from the previous *The Secret of the Whistler*. William Clemens (directing his final movie), veteran of other B-series such as The Falcon and Nancy Drew, became the latest director to be compared unfavorably to William Castle. Even though the series returned to the darkness of the criminal underworld and focused heavily on the world of corruption, the story seemed listless. Star Richard Dix played trucking company owner Steve Reynolds, a man framed for crimes he did not commit, so he is never a morally conflicted individual, as his best characterizations always were. Instead, this movie follows the B-Western formula of having a decent and hard-working man framed by the *outlaws* in an attempt to take over his business, which he refuses to allow them to have. In fact, the overly complicated script (the movie runs only 65 minutes or so) by Edward Bock and Raymond L. Schrock is one of the main problems. If the screenplay were simplified, it would prove to be less frustrating and more enjoyable. Even the mostly night-lit cinematography by Vincent Farrar is competent but never inspired. In most *Whistler* entries we have at least one or two major sequences that are superb examples of suspenseful or spooky cinematography, but here a few minor sequences are deftly handled in that manner.

As the whistling shadow of the Whistler appears, walking past trucks bearing the insignia for the Star Interstate Trucking Company (the operation owned and ran by Steve Reynolds), we are told, "And tonight, near this lonely spot on the highway, in a small town, we find an unusual birthday celebration in full swing." Reynolds is celebrating the birthday of his fiancée Eileen Blair (Karen Morley), who runs the local café. Reynolds hopes to marry her and become stepfather to her son Tommy (Mark Dennis) once his struggling business prospers. His trucking company is the new competition to the corrupt, long-established trucking business in town. After one drink Steve leaves to make a delivery. Picking up a well-dressed hitchhiker, Reynolds makes small talk when the warning from the mysterious Whistler booms over the soundtrack. "Ordinarily you don't pick up hitchhikers, Steve. But with a warming drink under your belt and the memory of Eileen's kiss on your lips, you're feeling friendly toward everybody. It was only a moment's delay but those 60 seconds are going to change the whole pattern of your life!" A situation is put into motion. A young couple, the male driver obsessed with his girlfriend, speeds and weaves down the dark single lane highway. He forces Reynolds to divert his truck off the road, and the truck crashes into the lone service station at about the time that motorcycle

cop Don Parker (Regis Toomey) is stopping to make a phone call. Don has bad blood for Reynolds because he also loved and lost Eileen. Smelling the one drink on Reynolds' breath, Don plans to throw the legal book at him. At the same time the couple that caused the accident are long gone, and so is the hitchhiker. So Reynolds has to face a drinking and driving charge and is convicted to six months in jail, suspended, but he also loses his license for six months. After the trial Reynolds bumps into Don, who apologies to Reynolds, stating he was simply doing his job. But Eileen accuses her former beau of allowing personal feelings to affect his professional actions. And Reynolds, overheard by two other policemen, threatens Don by proclaiming that every dog has his day and his is coming.

Problems escalate when Reynolds' driver gets sick and cannot make a produce delivery that must be made that night. Reynolds' chief mechanic and confidant, Charlie Cook (John Kellogg), wishes he could drive a rig, but even with a suspended license, Reynolds is the only man available. Even when rival trucking owner Jerry Mason (Jim Bannon) makes another offer to buy Reynolds out, Reynolds refuses. Jerry leaves making a veiled threat, "I always try to get what I want in a nice way, first!" However, when making his delivery the truck's motor malfunctions, and when Reynolds pulls on the side of the highway to fix it, a man wearing an aviator's mask emerges from the rear of the truck and knocks Reynolds unconscious, running his rig backwards over motorcycle cop Don Parker, who pulled them over for excessive speed. The stranger vanishes after knocking out Reynolds, but the stranger drops his leather glove, a glove with a slit thumb.

The Whistler's voice returns to analyze the state of Reynolds' mind. "Yes, Don is dead! You didn't kill him Steve, but will anyone believe you?" Reynolds abandons the truck and runs to Nevada to hide out, assuming menial jobs and sleeping in cheap rooms and flop houses. The only two people he can trust are Eileen and Charlie. In one moody flop house sequence, pretending he is blind, wearing a floppy hat and dark glasses, he uses his cane to find bed #5, only to discover that the police, who flip on the lights, are checking out the place. But the disguise works and one policeman even wishes him well. But the suspense, aided by Vincent Farrar's shadowy photography, reminds us of earlier, superior entries. Eating at a bar/restaurant the next day, Reynolds, still in disguise, overhears Jerry Mason talk to a few shady criminals and they speak of dropping off stolen cars at his trucking agency. Everything is pointing to the conclusion that since Reynolds would not sell out to rival Mason, that Mason put the frame on Reynolds to get him out of the way.

The Whistler's narration returns. "And so a fugitive slinks back under the cover of darkness, clinging to the slim hope that an old glove and a man with a missing thumb will help him prove his innocence." Reynolds returns to Eileen's place to ask her and Tommy for help, to be on the lookout for a man with a missing thumb. He tells Eileen he will be staying with buddy Charlie. However, waitress Mabel Sands (Bernadene Hayes), looking and acting shifty, tries to listen in on the conversation in the next room. And Tommy notices her spying.

From this point on, the plot becomes overly complex. Charlie, citing Reynolds' trucking company going belly-up, seeks employment working for rival Mason,

The killer forgets his glove... and a fistful of diamonds!

Steve Reynolds (Richard Dix) gets girlfriend Eileen (Karen Morley) to open her cafe safe and give him the glove.

but is he working on his own or working with Reynolds to get information from the Mason organization that could clear his buddy? Charlie gets a job parking cars since Mason already has enough mechanics, but Charlie parks one car that is driven by a criminal type wearing gloves similar to the lost glove Reynolds found. Charlie reports back to his friend that the man he saw does not have a thumb on his right hand, and that four stolen cars have been dropped off. When Reynolds wants to phone the police, Charlie suggests they pick up the missing thumb man first. Reynolds goes to see Eileen who is hiding the glove in her safe, but the police arrive and Reynolds has to sneak out the back window before he can get the glove.

But in a clever wink to the original movie in the series, the police spot Tommy reading the same book on necrophobia that appeared in *The Whistler* (read by ruthless hit man J. Carrol Naish).

Reynolds arrives at Mason's office to find the safe open and Mason dead. As he bends down to further examine the crime scene, the shadow of a man behind Reynolds knocks him unconscious, searches him and flees. When Reynolds awakens, he finds Charlie slowly exiting a parked car outside, rubbing the back of his head as well.

Returning to Eileen's place to fetch the glove, Eileen shows him a fake glass thumb within the glove, and the glass is filled with stolen diamonds. Tommy catches Mabel snooping once again and tells Reynolds and his mom. Mabel then informs Eileen that her brother is sick and that she has to leave work early, and Reynolds realizes that she must be connected to the man they are after. Reynolds borrows Eileen's car to follow her and hopefully lead him to the man who owns the glove and the stolen diamonds. Of course it turns out the guilty man is Reynolds' friend Charlie. Don, the policeman who was crushed and killed by the mysterious masked driver, recognized Charlie as being a member of a gang that pulled off a diamond heist on the East Coast (but the gems were never recovered). Don was blackmailing Charlie. It was the disguised Charlie who hid in the back of Reynolds' truck, overpowered Reynolds and killed Don by backing the truck over him. The only unresolved problem is for Charlie to find the missing glove and get his diamonds back. Unfortunately, Reynolds confides in Charlie one time too often and Reynolds finds himself tied up at Mabel's apartment, again without the missing glove. Reynolds is forced to write a note to Eileen, to get her to come to Mabel's place with the glove, but the clever Tommy tips off the police who arrive at Mabel's a few minutes after Eileen does. Charlie is shot and Reynolds' name is cleared. With the reward money that he knew nothing about, Reynolds can finally get his trucking business restarted and afford to marry Eileen.

On a happy note, the Whistler ends the movie with, "Yes, Steve, you were lucky. Stopping for 60 seconds to give a stranger a lift did change the pattern of your entire life. It may have ended in disgrace or even death, but fate was kind to you." It's been a while since the Whistler spoke of fate, but good karma led to a satisfying conclusion.

The Thirteenth Hour returns the *Whistler* series to the criminal foundation on which it began, and the cine-matography once again featured a small town on the outskirts of society bathed in darkness and shadow. The film's major flaw concerned an overly complex plot that featured perhaps one or two too many twists and turns. Instead of having Steve Reynolds become a man morally conflicted as is usual in the ser-ies, we find Reynolds to be the victim of a cruel frame, so the usual theme of moral conflict is nowhere to be found. It might be surprising initially to discover that Reynolds' best friend Charlie is the man who undermines Reynolds at every opportunity, but upon a second viewing we have specific clues that Charlie has been playing Reynolds. After Charlie gets Reynolds to go to Mason's office, he expects him to have the glove on his person (remember, the sudden arrival of the police at Eileen's place prevented Reynolds from getting the glove). After knocking Reynolds unconscious at Mason's company, Charlie (as a shadow) goes through his pockets fully expecting to find the glove and leave Reynolds to take blame for the death of Mason, his business rival (and it has been established that Reynolds needed money). So when the glove was not found, Charlie pretends to have been clunked over the head by the same man who clunked Reynolds. And remember, when Reynolds wanted to phone the police, it was Charlie who convinced him not to phone just yet. And at the end, when Reynolds gathers Charlie to go to Mabel's place, it is Charlie who insists he take his own gun. Even though *The Thirteenth Hour* is back on track stylistically, the film's script undermines the otherwise good features this entry offers.

Finally, the *Whistler* series came to an end with *The Return of the Whistler* in 1948, without perennial star Richard Dix. However the co-star of *The Secret of the Whistler*, Michael Duane, who played the artist boyfriend of artist model

Kay Morrell, steps into the driver's seat by graduating to star billing in this final entry. Director D. Ross Lederman (who directed B-entries in the *Lone Wolf* and *Boston Blackie* series before graduating to television) worked from a Cornell Woolrich story (*The Mark of the Whistler* was also based upon a Woolrich story) with the screenplay written by Edward Boch and Maurice Tombragel. For the first time in the series, cinematographer Philip Tannura returns (he photographed *Mysterious Intruder* two years earlier) and his camerawork most resembles the old dark house and film noir genres stylistically. Even though by 1948 B-mystery/detective series were waning, this final entry, although sadly missing the morally conflicted characters crafted by Richard Dix, was a step up from the last two entries starring Richard Dix. The final movie focused once again on dank mystery, ladies in distress and evil authority figures. The series could not have ended on a higher note.

In the dark of night, torrential rain falls as lightning cracks across the sky. The shadow of the Whistler walks across the rain-ravished streets. "And here tonight driving through this rain-swept countryside are two young people about to embark upon the greatest adventure of their lives. Whether for better or for worse, only time will tell." A speeding car carrying two eager young people arrives at the justice of the peace to be married. Handsome Ted Nichols (Michael Duane) and beautiful French bride-to-be Alice Dupres (Lenore Aubert, who was the female scientist from *Abbott and Costello Meet Frankenstein*) talk about their hopes and dreams. Even though Nichols made an appointment in advance, the justice of the peace is weather bound in another city and won't be back until the morning. A mysterious man parks his car next to Nichol's car, jumps out, pops Nichol's hood and fiddles with the engine. Nichols tells the woman that they will return in the morning to see the justice, and they head out to a recommended hotel, the only one in this small-town burgh. Even though the car sputters and needs repair, it hobbles to the hotel anyway. The desk attendant Anderson (Olin Howland) tells the couple the hotel is full. But for $20 under the table (no need to sign the register he says) Anderson can put them up for the night in a room needing remodeling. Discovering that the couple is not yet married, Anderson demands that Nichols leave and Nichols tells Alice that he will go to the mechanic down the road and sleep in the car. He promises to return early tomorrow.

"This is not the way you planned your honeymoon, is it Ted? It is only a few more hours until you and Alice will be united forever." The Whistler's voice is ominous.

New series star Michael Duane (as Ted Nichols) holds a gun on two people who *may* be John Barkley (James Cardwell) and his elderly mother (Ann Shoemaker).

The next morning Ted arrives at the hotel and finds a new desk clerk on duty and the room that Alice occupied now vacant and being painted. He demands to see the night duty clerk Anderson, who sleeps in back. He tells Ted that Alice left the hotel about half an hour after he left. When Ted roughs up Anderson because he cannot believe his bride-to-be would desert him (being a French girl, she did not know the country), the hotel manager intervenes. If Nichols agrees to stay away from the hotel, no charges will be pressed against him.

About this time a well-dressed man from the hotel lobby introduces himself to Nichols as a private detective, Gaylord Traynor (James Cardwell), who perhaps can help him find his girl Alice. Traynor suggests going back to his apartment to get a few photos of Alice to share with the police. When the two drive back, Nichols has the opportunity to provide the movie audience (and Traynor) with Alice's history.

Surprisingly, Nichols only met Alice for the first time two weeks ago. Alice, tired and exhausted, was walking through the brush and hurt her ankle. Alice seemed afraid to go back home; all she wanted was a drive to the bus station to get to the city. But gallant Nichols rescued her and bandaged her ankle. Too late for Alice to catch a bus, Nichols allowed Alice to spend the night on his couch and she left to find a place of her own the next day. But by that night she returned to Nichols to move in, citing every place in town was occupied. Alice complained that Nichols was too nice and she wanted to return to France, that America frightened her. Nichols planned to begin a six-month job in Brazil, starting next week, and he wanted Alice to housesit for him. Alice told him her American husband died in combat on their wedding night. After Alice's mother died, she had no one and came to America to find the surviving relatives of her husband—an aunt and several cousins. One of the cousins sexually assaulted her one night. And these are the people she fled. Alice told Nichols she must leave because she sensed the physical attraction he had for her, but immediately he asked her to marry him. All the while Nichols relates this past history to Traynor, the detective grills him in subtle ways. The final incident conveyed concerns a mysteriously cloaked burglar that broke into the bedroom as Alice slept (Nichols now sleeps on the sofa) but was scared off as he searched the drawers for some unknown article. Nichols, who never saw the intruder, tried to convince Alice she was only dreaming. Traynor predicts when they arrive at the apartment that all of Alice's things will be gone and she will have left him a note.

Instead, the men find no letter and Alice's clothes are intact. But finding Alice's marriage license to her first husband, Nichols discovers that her married name was Barkley and Nichols finds a pile of photos, a few showing Alice and her former husband John. Nichols recalls a Barkley house up at the lake where he rents a cabin, and while Nichols is deep in thought, Traynor sucker-punches him, takes the marriage license, photos and flees. The Whistler's commentary returns, as does his shadow—"You walked right into that one, didn't you Ted? But now you know exactly where you stand. There are others, shall we say, interested in Alice. And that marriage certificate must be of great importance to someone. That's why Traynor went through all this trouble to get it away from you. You're on your own now Ted, and with no time to spare!"

Nichols barges into the Barkley household and meets an elderly woman and man who claim they are John Barkley and his mother. That is the same John Barkley who is married to Alice. Holding a gun on the pair, Nichols demands to speak with Alice. Barkley takes his time explaining things to Nichols, telling Nichols that the reports of his death overseas were premature, and that because of the shock, Alice sometimes has lapses, Barkley calls them spells, where she believes that he is dead and she is free to romance and marry once again. Barkley admits that Traynor was working for him. Nichols calls Barkley a liar, but Barkley takes Nichols upstairs to hear all this from Alice's lips. Quiet and in bed, Alice apologizes but confirms everything that Barkley stated was the truth. When Nichols is hustled out of the room, a mysterious man, hidden in the closet, emerges, holding a pistol on Alice. Another younger woman also enters and tells Alice the show is over. Obviously, these are the cousins who are creating the lie that the imposter Barkley is Alice's husband. The man is only her cousin. If Alice marries Nichols the estate will fall into her hands and the in-laws lose everything. The con artists sold the estate and plan to leave tonight. The so-called mother, actually the late husband's aunt, has plans for Alice—her involuntary commitment to a sanatorium.

Nichols finds Alice's passport prov-ing when she first came to the United States. The Whistler returns to sum the situation up. "So Alice actually came to this country only about three weeks ago. She hasn't been here for several years, as Barkley wants you to believe. That changes everything Ted, doesn't it? Something seems very wrong, but after what Alice just told you, you can't go to the police. You got to find out for yourself."

Private Detective Traynor, having enlarged the family photos of Alice and her husband, discovers that the Barkley that hired him is not he same man shown in the photos, so Traynor admits to his secretary he was working for the wrong side. Traynor immediately decides to figure things out and go directly to the police.

With the aide of the Barkley grounds keeper, Nichols follows the family to the Woodland Sanatorium, pretending to be a depressed headache sufferer in order to see the attending physician, Dr. Grantland, on short notice. Once admitted to the hospital (while being escorted to his room Nichols passes Alice's room and hears the girl's frantic pleas inside), Nichols snoops around, frees the straitjacketed Alice and finds he and Alice cleared when Traynor arrives on the scene with the police, who now know the truth. The movie ends with Alice and Nichols returning to the same justice of the peace, to finally be married.

For the final time the voice of the Whistler concludes the movie talking about his favorite topic, fate. "You certainly were lucky Ted. It might have ended differently, with you and Alice worlds apart, but fate, this time, was on your side."

This edition of the *Whistler* series returned to the basics of the boilerplate mystery story. We have a beautiful woman disappear on the day of her supposed marriage. We have dead husbands who turn up alive, but again, is the self-professed husband actually the husband? We have innocent parties committed to sanatoriums. We have shady private detectives whose motives are not clear. We have the sexy French bride-to-be who might be innocent or she might be insane. The photography of Philip Tannura is crisp and suggestively moody in the major sequences. But, except for the opening nighttime drenching rain marriage sequence, Tannara this time does not get the opportunity to paint with such a noir-ish palette. Instead

Frightened Alice Dupres (Lenore Aubert) is surrounded by the relatives of her late husband that want the family inheritance, something they won't get if Alice re-marries.

we have sequences of opulence at the Barkley house, bright contrast at the hotel (with that strange little room) and creepy claustrophobia in the halls at the sanatorium at the end. Once again the plot is thick with suspense and mystery, and we the audience have to figure out who is who and what everyone's motives are. Poor Alice, perhaps she's a sympathetic woman who lost her husband on her wedding night, or, perhaps, a mentally disturbed pathological liar who does not remember that she is indeed already married. This time the plotting is tight as a drum, well paced and ultimately delivers the goods. It is sad that the eight movie series ended on such a high note without Richard Dix. *The Return of the Whistler* is a return to form and the series ends most satisfyingly.

Rudolph C. Flothow produced all eight *Whistler* entries, and he was an experienced B-programmer producer. He also produced features for the *Crime Doctor* series, the *Lone Wolf* series, the *Boston Blackie* series, as well as producing *The Phantom* and first *Batman* serials, the feature *The Monster and the Ape* and television series such as *Ramar of the Jungle* and *The New Adventures of Charlie Chan*. Even over five years, Flothow maintained a consistency of quality, even though the *Whistler* series was at heart a diverse anthology series that

skirted many different avenues of crime. But the one constant was our shadowy narrator the Whistler himself, whose ironic psychological undercurrents often returned to the topic of fate and how fate treats the protagonist at the movie's end. The cloaked, bathed-in-shadow figure, with the distinct whistling tune and that authoritative yet commanding voice, was the glue that held everything together. That and the starring performances of the aging Richard Dix, at times portraying romantic leads even though the actor was well into his 50s. But Dix's likability, even when playing conflicted and mortally bankrupt characters, made him an object of focus in every *Whistler* movie, until his retirement after the seventh entry. At just a little over an hour each, these mysteries of moral ambiguity managed to frighten us, confound us and keep us on the edges of our seats (though admittedly one or two entries came up a little short). And for a low-budget Columbia mystery series programmer, audiences could not ask for anything more.

In July 2014 none of the *Whistler* series is available on legitimate home DVD release, but gray market versions exist for those brave enough to chance a purchase of dubious quality. I cannot venture to comment whether fate would be kind to you for purchasing the series in this manner.

Fred MacMurray: Hollywood's Invisible Legend

by Nicholas Anez

"How could I have known that murder can sometimes smell like honeysuckle?"
Walter Neff, *Double Indemnity*

In his study of the 1944 classic film, *Double Indemnity*, author Richard Schickel (BFI Publishing; 1992) writes of Fred MacMurray's performance: "His is, I think, one of the greatest performances in the history of American movies." Schickel adds that, "Because he remains typed in everyone's mind as just another agreeable face, [the performance] is the least acknowledged of them."

This, in a nutshell, encapsulates the career of Fred MacMurray. It was a career that spanned more than dec-

Remember the Night, darkly romantic, becomes a voyage of self-discovery for both Lee (Barbara Stanwyck) and John (Fred MacMurray), in this Christmas delight.

ades and 80 movies, including starring roles in dramas, romances, musicals, mysteries, comedies and Westerns. He also found the time to star in one of the longest-running situation comedies in the history of television. If he displayed his superb skill only in a handful of movies, it is because most of his roles were not very challenging. As a result, he was consistently taken for granted and usually dismissed as an affable leading man. As evident from Mr. Schickel's statement, such an assessment disregards not just one but several exceptional performances.

Fred MacMurray was born in 1908 in Kankakee, Illinois but, shortly thereafter, his family moved to Wisconsin where he spent most of his formative years in the town of Beaver Dam. He attended Carroll College in Wisconsin but left school to begin his show business career as a musician, playing the saxophone in local bands and occasionally singing. He appeared as extras in three 1929 movies but had more success on Broadway, where he had roles in two plays, including a fairly prominent one in *Roberta* in 1933. A talent scout from Paramount Pictures arranged a screen test and, in 1934, MacMurray signed a contract with Paramount. The studio loaned him to RKO for his first credited role in *Grand Old Gal*. Claudette Colbert, one of Paramount's leading stars, was looking for a leading man for her next movie, *The Gilded Lily*, and, after seeing him in the RKO film, chose him to co-star with her. His career was off and running.

From 1935 to 1939, MacMurray appeared in 22 movies and established himself as an actor who seemed comfortable in virtually every genre. His

Once away from the corrupting "big city" in *Remember the Night*, the characters created by MacMurray and Stanwyck soften and become nurturing and caring.

Mad About Movies #9   41

Fred MacMurray and Joan Crawford in the thriller, *Above Suspicion*

films include comedies (*Hands Across the Table*), dramas (*Alice Adams*), musicals (*Swing High, Swing Low*), action films (*Men with Wings*) and Westerns (*The Texas Rangers*). He co-starred with some of the most popular actresses in Hollywood during its Golden Age, and many of them—including Carole Lombard and Madeleine Carroll, as well as Claudette Colbert—appeared with him several times. They enjoyed working with him not only because of his talent, but because he consistently displayed a total lack of ego. His portrayals also reflected this type of modesty that increased his likability among audiences. However, as popular as many of these films were, MacMurray's roles were not demanding and he just provided his usual engaging performance. The public liked him while critics considered him competent but unexceptional.

The 1940s initially promised more of the same. Between 1940 and 1943, MacMurray remained very busy and starred in 14 movies. *Remember the Night* (1940), his first film with Barbara Stanwyck, stands out among this crowded field. MacMurray plays John Sargent, an assistant district attorney, who prosecutes Lee Leander (Stanwyck) for stealing jewelry. He has a track record for winning cases, especially against women, and postpones the case until after Christmas to ensure a conviction. But when he realizes that she will have to spend the holidays in jail, he arranges bail for her. Lee is a tough cookie, at least on the surface, but she is suspicious of John's motives. But John is just doing a good deed to ease his conscience. However, when he learns that she is from his home state of Indiana, he offers to take her to her mother's residence. This begins a journey of self-discovery for both of them as they gradually fall in love

Remember the Night is a romantic drama with a dark undercurrent. Indeed, Lee's visit home has a definite film noir tinge. But the film also has some elements of the screwball comedy, at least during the early part of the road trip. The film veers smoothly from comedy to drama and even has a few musical interludes. But it eventually evolves into a sentimental story about the importance of family upbringing and the meaning of Christmas. However, the sentiment is grounded in reality. Though John's family has a heartwarming effect upon Lee, she is still facing possible imprisonment. John has to decide between either convicting Lee or ruining his career. This quandary leads to a self-sacrificial act by both John and Lee. Thanks to the deft handling of Preston Sturges' script by director Mitchell Leisen, the film's diverse parts all jell beautifully, right up to the concluding courtroom scene. The ending is not as happy as it could be but it is realistic and logical; it is also uplifting and satisfying.

MacMurray consistently underplays and allows Stanwyck to dominate most of the dramatic scenes, which she does with her usual expertise. Initially, John appears to be an ambitious bureaucrat who is more interested in obtaining convictions than justice. But MacMurray utilizes his intrinsic amiability to reveal his character's softer side under the surface. He also displays his comedic talent quite effectively in some of the early scenes and then develops into a romantic leading man as his character gradually falls in love. And, in the concluding courtroom sequence, he gets the opportunity to display some real dramatic capability as John is faced with his moral dilemma. *Remember the Night* is a hidden gem, just waiting to be re-discovered as an annual Christmas treat.

Fred MacMurrany and Paulette Goddard from *The Forest Rangers*

Walter Neff (Fred MacMurray) gets friendly with seductress Phyllis (Barbara Stanwyck).

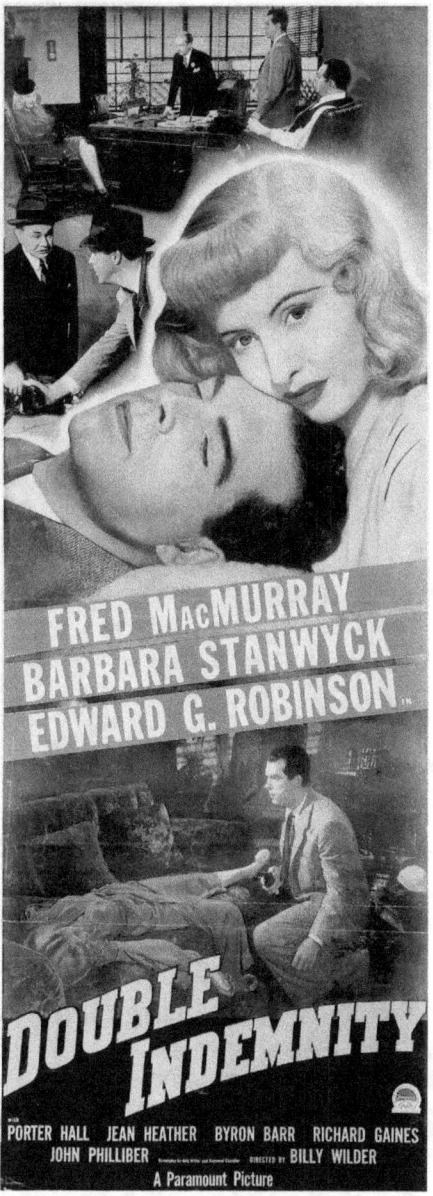

In the dozen or more films that followed, MacMurray continued to display a likable and deceptively effortless screen presence. Most were romantic comedies (*No Time for Love, One Night in Lisbon*, etc), but he also made action films (*The Forest Rangers*), thrillers (*Above Suspicion*) and historical dramas (*Virginia*). Many of his comedies seemed interchangeable as he romanced leading ladies and tossed off witty one-liners in his inimitable style. In all of them, he presented the image of an All-American male, the kind of person who represented such values as trustworthiness and integrity. His relaxed manner and natural charm made him so popular that, in 1942, he was reportedly the highest-paid actor in Hollywood.

In 1944, MacMurray starred in four movies, three of them providing routine roles where he displayed his typical aptitude. But one 1944 movie—his second with Barbara Stanwyck—was something else entirely. Director Billy Wilder offered him a character that was quite the contrary to his usual screen image and, after a period of indecision, he accepted and made motion picture history.

In *Double Indemnity*, MacMurray plays Walter Neff, an insurance salesman who is seduced by Phyllis Dietrichson (Stanwyck) into killing her husband. Walter thinks that he can get away with murder but he doesn't count on the appearance of the company's claims inves-tigator, Barton Keyes (Edward G. Robinson), who is always on the alert for any kind of mischief, including murder. Unlike virtually every other character MacMurray had played in all of his previous movies, Walter is a horrible person. He makes love to a married woman and he betrays the man who is probably his only friend. After committing one murder, he kills again. This is not the kind of role that audiences were accustomed to seeing MacMurray play.

Audiences will hate Walter Neff—unless he has qualities that suggest that he is not innately evil but weak enough to be susceptible to evil. This is where MacMurray's skill is utilized. In the beginning, Walter's obvious despair and pain invite sympathy before he starts to tell the story of his downfall. By his projection of emotional and physical suffering as he speaks into the Dictaphone, he is able to bring to Neff an air of pathos, if not tragedy. He initially makes Walter despicable but, after the murder, subtly suggests a gradual development of guilt for his character. As Walter confirms his alibi in his apartment, he looks morose, implying that his conscience is beginning to re-surface. When he returns to Keyes' office to find out if the crafty investigator suspects him, he listens quietly as Keyes expresses his belief in his friend's innocence because of his trust in him. MacMurray doesn't register any obvious change in his expression, but his fixed glare communicates unmistakable shame and regret.

Eventually, anger replaces Walter's guilt when he realizes that he has been duped. From that moment on, although he plans for a way out of the death trap in which he finds himself, MacMurray makes it clear through his air of resignation that Walter wants to die. As he lures Phyllis into the trap he has set for her, no urgency registers in his voice; there is only acceptance of what he hopes will be his fate. When Phyllis shoots him,

Fred MacMurray and Barbara Stanwyck in a studio publicity pose for *Double Indemnity*

no surprise appears on his face because his expression clearly reflects that this is what he wanted. And in the last sequence, his tortured face conveys some degree of relief when he looks over his shoulder and sees Keyes in the doorway of his office. It is clear that, as painful as it was for him, he had to personally confess to Keyes before trying to reach the border. He obviously felt that he owed this much to his friend. Such complex emotions, though not expressed in the dialogue, are all in MacMurray's expression, tone and demeanor.

The key to this successful portrayal is MacMurray's internal absorption of his character. He never resorts to overt displays of emotion to express what he is feeling. He initially suggests a brash self-confidence but, as the story unfolds, his manner reveals a gradual obliteration of that same arrogance. Though greed and passion consume him in the beginning, slight changes in his manner suggest a gradual absorption of doubt and remorse. MacMurray conveys superbly such inner turmoil by unmistakable differences in his demeanor, including not only the way he conducts himself in the presence of others, but also in his manner of speaking. As he relates his story, the increasing despondency in his tone suggests that his voice—like his footsteps earlier in the story—is that of a dead man. This powerful and persuasive performance is the centerpiece of the movie, despite the equally fine portrayals of his two co-stars.

The Academy of Motion Picture Arts and Sciences bestowed seven Academy Award nominations upon *Double Indemnity* (though it did not win in any category) but overlooked MacMurray's performance. Studio politics were definitely a factor in this omission, since he had not renewed his contract with Paramount and had signed with 20th Century Fox. In view of this, Paramount put its weight behind Bing Crosby (who had starred with MacMurray in the 1938 musical, *Sing You Sinners*) for his role in *Going My Way*. No offense to Crosby, but his role in that crowd-pleaser was tailored particularly for his screen persona. Though the Academy nominated Stanwyck for her memorable performance, it disregarded MacMurray. (The Academy also ignored Edward G. Robinson's outstanding portrayal of Keyes; incredulously, the inimitable Robinson also never received even a nomination, but that is a subject for another article.)

Curiously, the Academy nominated Crosby's co-star Barry Fitzgerald for Best Actor and also for Best Supporting Actor for the same role! The other Best Actor nominations were Cary Grant for *None But the Lonely Heart*, Charles Boyer for *Gaslight* and Alexander Knox for *Wilson*. The Academy rewarded Grant—but not MacMurray—for playing against type. Boyer was suitably menacing but, though Knox is a good actor, he gave a dull performance in an equally dull film, only receiving a nomination because the movie was considered prestigious. Fitzgerald was his usual adorable self but, since he was nominated in both categories, he was a shoo-in to win the lesser award, which he did. Accordingly, Crosby won the Best Actor award while MacMurray, who gave the best performance of the year, got the shaft.

Lieutenant Tom Keefer (MacMurray), a nasty piece of work, from *The Caine Mutiny*

(Oscars were often a reflection of a star's popularity. In 1944, motion picture exhibitors put Crosby at the top of Quigley's Annual List of Box Office Champions and also voted him Number One for the next four years. MacMurray never made the list and, throughout his career, always seemed to fly just under the radar.)

After this superlative performance, MacMurray returned to frothy roles in mostly unremarkable movies. As an example of his versatility, after *Double Indemnity*, he starred in two comedies, including the very funny *Murder, He Says*, in which he displays command of slapstick comedy timing. This role was about as different from Walter Neff as could be imagined—and yet he did both roles with equal proficiency. Nevertheless, it would be only after 10 years and 20 more movies at various studios that he finally got another challenge. During the period, *Smoky*, a 1946 Western for Fox, and *The Egg and I*, a 1947 comedy for Universal-International, were huge commercial hits and kept his name among the most bankable. By the early 1950s, however, his career showed signs of slippage as the quality of his movies declined. In 1953, he co-starred with Barbara Stanwyck for the third time in *The Moonlighter*, a sub-par 3-D Western that they both should have avoided. But then in 1954, he won another genuinely demanding role when he was cast as Lieutenant Tom Keefer in *The Caine Mutiny*.

An all-star cast headlines *The Caine Mutiny*, one of the most critically and commercially successful films of the year. Humphrey Bogart gives a brilliant performance as the unstable Captain Queeg, whose increasing inability to function due to the stress of command during World War II is exacerbated by the disloyalty of his subordinates. Jose Ferrer is compelling as Barney Greenwald, the defense attorney who reluctantly completes the destruction of Queeg begun by the mutineers. Van Johnson is also convincing as Executive Officer Lt. Steve Maryk, who only wants to do what is right but is used as a pawn by the film's real villain. And that villain, Communications Officer Lt. Tom Keefer, showcases Fred MacMurray with just the right amount of smug cruelty.

Keefer is a glib and witty observer of the facts of life aboard the small minesweeper, the *U.S.S. Caine*. But beneath his sophisticated veneer is a manipulative cynic who hates the Navy and considers himself superior to everyone else. He views the war as an intrusion into his comfortable life and remains above his surroundings by writing a novel. He resents Queeg because of his social inferiority and, detecting that the captain is on the verge of a breakdown, proceeds to push him over that edge. He instigates the subject of Queeg's paranoia and plants the seeds of suspicion within Maryk and Ensign Keith (Robert Francis) that eventually lead to the mutiny. And then, when Maryk and Keith need him to support their version of the events that he precipitated, Keefer betrays them. He is a nasty piece of work whose hypocrisy is fully exposed in the denouement.

MacMurray captures perfectly all of these qualities with a terrific portrayal that is as complex as his character. Initially, he creates a persuasive portrait of cerebral arrogance. However, as the tension aboard the *Caine* intensifies, it gradually becomes clear that Keefer's sense of superiority conceals feelings of insecurity. When he and his co-conspirators visit Admiral Halsey's flagship to report Queeg's bizarre behavior, Keefer realizes that he doesn't have the courage to follow through with his plan. Keefer's expression of embarrassment as he confesses his cowardice is so pitiable that he invites sympathy for his character, despite his culpability. Unfortunately, it is too late

Fred MacMurray, as the corrupted police detective, clutches Kim Novak close to him in *Pushover*, "a story of temptation," as the lobby declares.

to stop the course of events that he has caused and he subsequently exposes his treachery at the court-martial. As he lies to save his own skin, he is mixed with shame and self-loathing. MacMurray's multifaceted portrayal splendidly reveals all of these feelings—from malice and pompousness to spinelessness and humiliation.

The Academy nominated *The Caine Mutiny* for seven Academy Awards (but it did not win any Oscars), including Humphrey Bogart for Best Actor. The other nominees for Best Actor were Marlon Brando for *On the Waterfront*, James Mason for *A Star is Born*, Dan O'Herlihy for *Adventures of Robinson Crusoe* and—again—Bing Crosby for *The Country Girl*. Since MacMurray's name was billed fourth among the stars of *Caine*, Academy members might have considered his role a supporting one, even though Keefer is the real counterpoint to Queeg. The nominees in the Best Supporting Actor category included three actors from *On the Waterfront*—Karl Malden, Lee J. Cobb and Rod Steiger—along with Edmond O'Brien for *The Barefoot Contessa*. Tom Tully was the fifth nominee for his role as the captain who is replaced by Queeg in *Caine*. Tully was a good character actor but his portrayal is not exceptional and was not required to be. Once again, MacMurray's consummate skill was ignored.

Following *The Caine Mutiny*, MacMurray played a role that was reminiscent of Walter Neff in a movie entitled *Pushover*. He was very good as an honorable police detective who turns crooked because of a duplicitous woman. But co-star Kim Novak was no Barbara Stanwyck and director Richard Quine was no Billy Wilder. Nevertheless, the film showed that he could once more rise to the occasion and was more than believable as a rogue cop.

Clifford Groves (MacMurray) lives a life of quiet desperation, caught between his controlling wife (Joan Bennett) and an emotional fling with the other woman (Barbara Stanwyck).

By 1955, Fred MacMurray had been a major star for two decades so it was perhaps inevitable that he would eventually be relegated to second features. He made his first B Western, *At Gunpoint*, and though he was never comfortable in the saddle, he proved to be quite credible in this feature as well as in six more bottom-of-the-bill oaters over the next five years. He brought the same kind of sincerity to these movies as he did to his more prestigious films, and some of them—such as *Gun for a Coward* and *Good Day for a Hanging*—are excellent examples of the B-genre.

In 1956, MacMurray briefly returned to A-features when he co-starred for the fourth and last time with Barbara Stanwyck in Douglas Sirk's *There's Always Tomorrow*. This is an underrated domestic drama with fine performances from its three stars, including Joan Bennett—who played opposite him 20 years earlier in *Thirteen Hours by Air*—as his wife. On the surface, the movie sounds like a standard soap opera. However, following the credits, the rainstorm that follows a title card's description, done up in ornate print of "sunny California," indicates that the film's title may be equally deceptive.

Fred MacMurray portrays Clifford Groves, a loving husband and father whose wife and three children take him for granted. They are all so self-absorbed that they don't realize that they are depriving Cliff of any kind of emotional fulfillment. When former employee Norma Vale (Stanwyck) returns for a visit, Cliff sees an opportunity to regain the lost dreams of his youth. His two older children, sensing something is amiss, quickly interfere because they want their father to remain in the position that they have chosen for him. Cliff's identification with the toy robot in his factory implies a subconscious understanding that his family will always control his life. But, for a brief while, he pretends he is young again and that an escape exists for him. Though Norma has always loved him, she eventually forces him to accept the painful but obvious truth about himself. This leads to an ending that seemingly suggests happiness but, beneath the surface, implies a life of quiet desperation.

Cliff's inner conflicts make him a difficult character to portray, but MacMurray pulls it off quite expertly. He conveys genuine love for his family but yet suggests an underlying frustration that he cannot express overtly. He expresses passionate love for Norma that is also accompanied by frustration because he realizes that the relationship can never lead anywhere. Cliff's subconscious acceptance of his fate is obvious from MacMurray's expression of subdued resignation when he is at home or at work. It is confirmed by his combined expression of despair and relief when Norma rejects him. At the finale, his robot-like movements fully convey the impression of a man who will forever be trapped by the American dream. For Cliff, there will never be a tomorrow. This is a notably introspective and intelligent performance that shines.

Naturally, there was not even consideration for an Oscar nomination

C.C. Baxter (Jack Lemmon) hands over the key to his apartment to boss Jeff Sheldrake (MacMurray) in Billy Wilder's *The Apartment.*

for MacMurray. The film failed at the box-office, perhaps due to its subversive message about middle-class domesticity, and the Academy tends to reward only successful films. This was also the same year that the Academy members also ignored John Wayne's superb performance in *The Searchers,* Sterling Hayden's in *The Killing,* Jack Palance's in *Attack,* James Mason's in *Bigger Than Life,* Van Heflin's in *Patterns* and Kevin McCarthy's in *Invasion of the Body Snatchers.* So MacMurray was in good company.

From 1955 to 1958, MacMurray also starred in four episodes of television anthology series, such as *20th Century Fox Hour* and *Screen Director's Playhouse.* Consequently, he received many offers to star in his own series but he refused them all, not wanting to commit himself to a weekly grind. Besides, he was still receiving film offers for B-Westerns and it seemed that his career was destined to languish in that second-class genre. But then, in 1959, Walt Disney called him to play the harried father of a boy who turns into a canine in *The Shaggy Dog.* This comedy's enormous success brought him back to A-movies, especially since his humorous characterization of the dog-hating mailman was an essential factor in the film's appeal. MacMurray's distinct ability to credibly combine fantasy and reality is more than evident in this film (and it is an ability that some comics, such as Tim Allen, sorely lack; see the 2006 remake for proof.) While *The Shaggy Dog* was filling theaters and endearing him to family audiences, MacMurray received an offer to play a role that would alienate many of those same audiences. It was a role in which he would again excel.

In 1960, Billy Wilder again asked for MacMurray's services for the role of Jeff Sheldrake in his comedy-drama, *The Apartment.* Wilder sensed the ominous potential beneath the actor's amiable roles because this second collaboration with him produces another contemptible character—a selfish and unscrupulous corporate executive who casually uses and abuses people beneath him. C.C. Baxter (Jack Lemmon) is an ambitious low-level employee who allows executives, including Sheldrake, to use his apartment for their infidelities. Baxter falls for elevator operator Fran Kubelik (Shirley MacLaine), who is in love with Jeff.

Since audiences have to believe that Fran can truly love this scoundrel, Jeff must have attractive qualities. MacMurray conveys this charm while at the same time making it obvious to everyone except Fran that Jeff's attractiveness is purely superficial. When Fran gives Jeff a Christmas present, MacMurray projects callousness, flawlessly followed by fake concern, and then total indifference to the pain he has caused her. Jeff can pour on the warmth with such ease that, in the scene with his wife and children around the Christmas tree, audiences do not know if he is pretending with them as much as he is pretending with Fran. And this is exactly the impression that MacMurray wants to give, which makes his portrayal another marvelous performance.

This is getting to sound like a broken record, but here it goes again. *The Apartment* was a huge commercial success and received 10 Academy Award nominations (winning five, including Best Picture and Director). The Academy nominated both Lemmon and Maclaine, while third-billed MacMurray was missing in action. Though his role was equal in importance to the other two stars, it is possible that the Academy did not want to give all three stars Best Actor

Fred MacMurray, William Demarest, Don Grady, Stanley Livingston and Barry Livingston, part of the family cast of *My Three Sons.*

"Neddy the Nut" (MacMurray) steers the flying car from *Son of Flubber*.

of Medford College's losing basketball team. Once again, MacMurray's delightful portrayal was of invaluable assistance to making the movie a colossal box-office hit.

MacMurray makes the professor wacky but loveable. When his character explains the pseudo-scientific basis of his invention, he delivers his lines with genuine enthusiasm. And he has a special way of tilting his head and talking excitedly that is guaranteed to endear Ned to anyone, especially an increasingly exasperated Betsy. Yet the portrayal still contains a realistic foundation for the characterization; while children and adults laugh at his antics, adults also notice recognizable traits in his manner and behavior. A lesser actor (such as Robin Williams; see the 1996 remake for proof) could have made Ned a hackneyed cartoon character, but MacMurray avoids such a stereotype through his expert interpretation of the role. His creation of Professor Brainard is as delightful as other comedic roles that won Academy Award nominations, including Jack Lemmon and Doris Day who were nominated a couple of years earlier for their roles in, respectively, *Some Like It Hot* and *Pillow Talk*. But, of course, MacMurray wasn't even considered.

For the duration of his career, MacMurray made six more movies, five for Disney. These included the sequel, *Son of Flubber*, in which he brought "Neddy the Nut" back for a second round. And while he was starring in these films throughout the 1960s and early 1970s, he continued to appear weekly on television in *My Three Sons,* which remained consistently popular. This is quite a unique achievement for any actor. Although many other film stars of his era achieved subsequent success on the small screen (Robert Young and Robert Montgomery are good examples), they all more or less stopped acting in theatrical films. But MacMurray continued to star in movies while retaining small screen fame.

The following facts are an indication of MacMurray's appeal at this time. For the 1966-1967 television season, his series was still achieving high ratings. During this same period, he starred in two Disney movies (*Follow Me, Boys* and *The Happiest Millionaire*), both of which were commercial successes. Also, Disney re-released *The Shaggy Dog* and *The Absent-Minded Professor* as a profitable double-feature. After three decades in the business, MacMurray was quite possibly at the height of his popularity. (Still, he never earned a place on Quigley's Annual List of Box-Office Champions; he apparently was just as invisible to motion picture exhibitors as he was to the Academy.)

MacMurray's television series ended in 1972. The following year, he had his final starring film role in Disney's *Charley and the Angel*. After a couple of television movies, he appeared in the 1978 disastrous disaster movie *The Swarm,* but he understandably preferred to forget that error in judgment. He subsequently retired, though he remained a very popular Hollywood personality. He died in 1991.

Fred MacMurray's image is that of a lightweight actor whose easygoing, good-natured style made him a popular movie star. He displayed the ability to play comedy as well as drama with equal skill. He also proved to be a reliable romantic leading man as well as a credible Western actor. Nevertheless, despite his versatility, he was rarely given the chance to stretch his talents as an actor. Fortunately, he had occasional opportunities to play roles that required an actor of considerable depth. When presented with such a challenge, he lit up the screen with extraordinary performances. In those films, he displayed such an immense amount of talent that he must be regarded, not only as one of Hollywood's most amiable stars, but one of its finest actors.

nominations. So it follows that they might have considered him for the Best Supporting category. Well, an actor from the movie did receive such a nomination, but it was Jack Kruschen for his role as the kindly doctor next door. Like Tom Tully, Kruschen was good but it was not an exceptional portrayal. As far as the Academy was concerned, the actor playing Jeff must have been the invisible man.

After years of continuing to reject offers to do a television series, MacMurray accepted a proposal that was too good to refuse, primarily because he would work on the series for only three months a year. In 1960, he began starring in *My Three Sons* that would be a fixture on the small screen for an amazing 12 years, making him one of television's most popular stars. Shortly after he started appearing in living rooms every week as the quintessential devoted father, Walt Disney called upon him once again.

In 1961, MacMurray created a truly memorable comedy character when he played the eccentric title role in Disney's *The Absent-Minded Professor*. He plays Professor Ned Brainard who repeatedly misses his wedding because he is too busy (accidentally) developing a gravity-defying substance, Flubber, as in flying rubber. The professor uses Flubber to great effect. First he uses Flubber in his Model T, competing against the rival for his fiancée Betsy's affections. And secondly he uses Flubber under the shoes

GET YOUR KICKS ON ROUTE 66

by Steve Vertlieb

Since *Route 66* was shot on locations in major cities across the U.S.A., the production company arrived in huge vans which promoted the series and became a calling card for young fans who wanted to be close by while a specific episode was being shot in their city.

This essay began as a succession of comments and observations found at the on-line *Classic Horror Film Board* TV forum where, to my amazement, the usual fantasy-themed discussions had turned miraculously to an affectionate remembrance of the 1960s CBS Television series *Route 66,* starring Martin Milner and George Maharis. While I remain a lifelong fantasy/science fiction/horror buff, I continue to have a warm place in my heart reserved for this iconic buddy series about a pair of traveling friends who sewed their youthful oats along the legendary snaking series of highways known as Route 66. *Route 66* has always been, and will always be, my all time favorite TV series. My brother Erwin and I were lonely, messed up kids struggling to find our voice and identities when we first began watching *Route 66* in 1960 on CBS. Right from the very first episode, "Black November," we knew that we were in for something different. This opening salvo seemed, to us, to be shot out of a cannon. It was powerful, shocking and really quite scary. Here were these two young men traveling in the middle section of the country, stranded in what seemed another planet, stalked ... threatened ... and attacked by vicious backwoods Neanderthals right out of *Bad Day At Black Rock*. Alone, and at the mercy of these bullies and thugs, Tod Stiles and Buz Murdock fought to preserve their inherent decency, while fighting off the attacks of an insane mob mentality. We were hooked right from the beginning. This was television like we'd rarely, if ever, seen it before.

Route 66 appeared on series television at the tail end of a distinguished cycle of live telecast dramas, and the program owed much to the excitement and intensity of the decade that had preceded it. While the series was broadcast each week on film, its location shooting gave it a sense of momentous reality found nowhere else on the tube. The program had a semi-documentary sensibility (often hand-held cameras were used) and was, in many ways, the dramatic, if fictional, forerunner of many of today's most riveting reality programs. The gritty black-and-white photography added immeasurably to the overwhelming sense of reality. The show had a sense of both immediacy and urgency about it, and it was difficult at times to remember that it was, after all, a scripted series and not two real guys being followed across the U.S.A. The writing was taut, dramatic and often uncomfortably genuine. We never had the sense that it was written by a guy behind a desk in Beverly Hills. My brother and I had led relatively sheltered lives of youthful sensitivity, idealism and romantic desperation. This became our escape, if you will. It was our secret ticket to adventure, a passport shared by only the two of us in the comparatively safe passenger seats of our home living room. Erwin and I, in a sense, became Tod and Buz ... traveling the country vicariously in front of our television sets and sharing their exhilarating rite of passage. We grew up on the road, floating over the tires of a testosterone-driven Chevy Corvette.

While we'd known Martin Milner from films and television over the years, we'd never seen or heard of George Maharis. He was, for his time, perhaps the most exciting new star to emerge from the shadows. His was a raw, un-

with every moment of growth and the passage of miles. While Leonard's own *Naked City,* airing on ABC, contained much of the same idealism and growing pains as its fledgling younger sibling, the locations for the popular cop show were largely grounded inherently in and around New York City. Stiles and Murdock, however, were under no such geographical constraints. They were like brothers, sharing life's adventure on the road, finding maturity in their travels, free to move in whichever directions their whims and desires led them. The inspiration for the series reputedly came from a lunchtime conversation between Leonard and Silliphant in which Leonard recounted his early years as a penniless teenager hanging around with his best friend, who just happened to be wealthy. From that thread of a recollection came the birth of Tod Stiles, a rich kid whose father died, leaving him only a Corvette with which to survive. Buz Murdock was his streetwise buddy, tempting him to search out new experiences on the road. Leonard and Silliphant chose *The Searchers* as the title for their coming of age saga. Warner Bros. owned the title and it already had a high profile attachment to the classic 1956 Western directed by John Ford, starring John Wayne. Understandably, the studio refused to negotiate the title's loan, requiring a change of direction from the producers. They settled, instead upon *Route 66* for this would set the stage for the imaginary tableau upon which the youthful adventurers would set forth on a cross country voyage of self discovery. The list of actors and actresses who populated their journey read like a casting call of every aspiring star or veteran performer alive and working. Many of America's finest young dramatic actors learned and developed their craft while appearing on the road-exploring *Route 66*. These included Robert Redford, Robert Duvall, Martin Sheen, Edward Asner and James Caan.

We lived for each new experience on life's unfolding highway. Each new city, town and neighborhood across the United States provided Tod and Buz with physical and emotional challenges designed to test both their endurance and yearning early maturity. However, the moment of ultimate truth came for us in the summer of 1961 as the pair neared the

bridled talent that seemed too large for the small screen. He was an exciting new presence ... volatile ... uncontrollable ... and explosive. He came seemingly out of nowhere, and yet possessed much of the same Actor's Studio energy shared by Marlon Brando, James Dean, Frank Sinatra and other postwar actors finding meaning in their inner rage and torment. Maharis had appeared in some small roles in major films, most notably as a Jewish freedom fighter distrustful of Paul Newman's intentions in Otto Preminger's *Exodus* (1960). For his part, Milner had always played squeaky-clean boys next door in a succession of American films dating back to *Life With Father*. In the late fifties he'd begun taking on more edgy adult roles in such cutting-edge films as *The Sweet Smell Of Success* and *Marjorie Morningstar*.

The stories and issues populating the scripts of this adventurous series were often provocative, emotionally powerful and, on a purely instinctual level, deeply and profoundly poetic. Produced by Herbert B. Leonard, with the majority of the scripts written by Stirling Silliphant, and all the original music composed by Nelson Riddle, *Route 66* grew more fascinating

Eastern Coast of the United States, and it was announced that they would travel first to Baltimore and then Philadelphia to shoot two episodes on location. We were exhilarated to learn that our literary counterparts would be traveling to our neck of the woods. In mid-October 1961, Tod and Buz drove into the outskirts of Philadelphia. Our frustration turned achingly real when we learned that the brother of our next-door neighbor was the head of the local advertising company playing host to the cast and crew. Ed and Rose Sommers had been our neighbors for many years. Their kids had grown up alongside us. Ed's brother Allan Sommers was the unit publicist for the show while they were in town. It seemed only natural that Ed would arrange for us to meet our heroes by interceding on our behalf with his brother. Ed and Allan deemed intrusive what appeared as natural and fitting to us, as reality reared its ugly head, shutting us out of our dream. We might just as well have been any old "generic" fans hoping for a momentary glimpse of their idols. This would be a once in a lifetime experience and opportunity for us. We had to take matters into our own sweaty palms and plan a secondary course of action. We learned through the local newspapers that the cast was being housed at a popular motel just beyond the city limits. So Erwin and I cut school and took a bus to the Marriott Motor Hotel on City Line Avenue in Bala Cynwyd, just outside of Philadelphia. Our excitement grew quite palpable as we saw the many production trailers sitting conspicuously in the hotel parking lot. Walking into the lobby of the hotel (I was 14 years old ... Erwin three years younger), I noticed character actor Murray Hamilton sitting on a couch reading a newspaper. He was playing a doctor in the episode they were filming. We walked over to him and introduced ourselves. I doubt that anyone else in the lobby had any idea who he was. I think he was so taken by these two kids who knew his work that he invited us to sit down and talk with him. He was very kind, as I recall, and spent fully a half hour chatting with us about his career, working with Jimmy Stewart in both *The FBI Story* and *The Spirit Of St. Louis*, and working on *The Twilight Zone* opposite Ed Wynn. (He later played

Buz Murdock (George Maharis) and Tod Stiles (Martin Milner) pose with their iconic Chevy Chevette as they crossed the country each week, finding new adventures.

"The Mayor Of Shark City" in Steven Spielberg's *Jaws*.)

We walked out of the lobby and into the parking lot adjoining the Marriott restaurant and there, as we saw through the glass window, sat Martin Milner eating his breakfast all alone ... brooding and intense. He was deep in thought, lost in his character but he looked up to face us. We had evidently pulled him from the deep recess of an emotionally exhausting thought process back to seemingly mundane reality. Feeling intrusive, we backed away from the window and returned into the hotel lobby. There we saw George Maharis emerging from the elevator. We approached him and told him how much we loved the series. He was warm, outgoing and very friendly to us. We talked for a few moments, and he invited us to join him and the rest of the crew for the climactic shoot in downtown Philadelphia at the Ben Franklin Bridge. His enthusiasm for the day's schedule was infectious. We didn't have to be asked twice.

We took yet another bus back into the inner city and found the immense suspension bridge dangling imposingly over the skyline. Somewhat apprehensively, we climbed onto the walkway of the massive expanse until we reached its swaying epicenter. On the opposite walkway the technicians and cast of *Route 66* stood preparing to

Each new city, town and neighborhood across the U.S. provided Tod and Buz with physical and emotional challenges designed to test their endurance and maturity.

film the final dramatic moments of what would prove to be our favorite, most intensely personal episode of the entire series. Martin Milner, in later interviews, said that it was also his favorite episode of the show. Per the story, Tod had mistakenly swallowed a "mickey" intended for someone else. We watched as Tod, in drug-induced paranoia, threatened to jump from the bridge to his death in the raging traffic below. "Don't do it, buddy. I love you," cried Buz to his stricken friend. As Tod regains his senses, climbing precariously into the sheltering arms of his beloved friend and brother, the scene ended and the camera crew began disassembling their equipment. The ensemble began coming down from the bridge, and Erwin and I came down with them, meeting at the opening gateway. As George Maharis walked quickly down to the street, he saw us standing there and waved enthusiastically with his characteristic smile. It was a moment we would somehow never forget.

"The Thin White Line" aired over the CBS network during the second season of the show on December 8, 1961. That hour would become the program's crowning achievement for us. It was all about love, friendship and loyalty ... a recurring theme on the series, but never more passionately captured on film than in this magnificent episode. (As for George Maharis, his own personal favorite episode of the long running series was a story called "Even Stones Have Eyes," in which he is temporarily blinded after a construction accident. Sobbing sightless through the dispassionate reflection of a hospital window, he cries, "I want to see.")

Another memorable episode appealed to genre fans throughout the world. We rejoiced one memorable evening in late October 1962 as the series presented its joyous comedic salute to the world of monsters and madmen at Halloween. "Lizard's Leg And Owlet's Wing" was a delicious bit of fluff in which three of monsterdom's most ghoulish practitioners arrived at a Chicago hotel incognito to discuss ways and means of returning the horror film to its former illustrious resonance. Boris Karloff appeared in one last, incomparable moment as Frankenstein's Monster. Lon Chaney, Jr. appeared as his most enduring incarnation, The Wolf Man, while Peter Lorre laid humorous waste to his own most monstrous creation, appearing as ... well ... Peter Lorre. As delightful as this memorable thematic detour from the famous highway may have been, the series found its most significant and enduring voice in its unflinching dramatic writing and performances, offering unforgettable treatments of such sensitive topics as mental illness, drug addiction and racial harmony. *Route 66* became a beacon of searingly honest, often painful dissections of social injustice and the human condition.

Fantasy is a poor substitute for reality however. As powerful as their on screen relationship and chemistry was, something had gone terribly wrong behind the cameras. Maharis was growing restless and wanted to move on. Milner said in later interviews that he was shocked to learn that his co-star didn't like him. Whether that was perception or fact, Milner would later comment in an interview with *TV Guide*, "I thought the guy liked me." Obviously stung by gossip of a growing resentment on the part of his co-star, Milner became hurt and reclusive. On the set of "Even Stones Have Eyes," Maharis was called upon to jump into an icy stream in order to rescue actress Barbara Barrie. He caught a chill and ultimately grew sick with a case of hepatitis, subsequently missing a succession of episodes of the series due to confinement and hospitalization. He would *milk* this illness—it was later said—to remain off the set for numerous episodes at a time, perhaps trying to ignite a film career. Maharis denied these published accusations as ridiculous and false. Milner filmed episodes by himself, while the network did its best to put a hopeful spin on the situation. The producers changed the thrust of the series to reflect a mysterious hospitalization, while the writers scrambled to compose stories in which Tod would telephone his friend from various cities along the fabled route, vainly awaiting his return to their joint excursions. For a time, Maharis did return and the series appeared to be getting back on track. Herbert Leonard seemed unsympathetic to the actor's health issues, bowing to contractual pressure from CBS to fulfill completion of their scheduled slate of programs. When Maharis continued to miss episodes, Glenn Corbett eventually replaced him, but the magic was gone. Corbett was a decent actor who struggled vainly to fill the shoes of his predecessor, but he simply couldn't duplicate the raw charisma and magnetism of Maharis. The show continued uninspired for a time, and finally left the CBS schedule after four years. However, those first 2 ½ years were among the finest hours of dramatic series' writing and performance in the history of television ... and, for one brief, shining moment ... my brother and I were actually there.

With all the enthusiasm of youth and the excitement it provides, Buz and Tod gleefully confront another city in "Don't Count Stars."

People always ask me about the car. Well, if memory serves me ... and that was more than 50 years ago ... the car was only taken out of the van when it was going to be photographed for a pertinent shot. When not in use, it was generally hidden from prying eyes inside one of the massive transport tractor-trailer trucks that accompanied the company around the country. I may have observed the back of the Corvette sitting inside the truck, but I hope no one will ask me about its color. It's just been too long ago.

Incidentally, there's a fascinating blog by writer Karen Funk Blocher about the series at Route 66 News.com. It's actually a very depressing account of the rapid rise and fall of George Maharis and the circumstances leading to his eventual career decline. It isn't a secret that the actor was gay. Herbert B Leonard, the show's executive producer, hired Maharis because he felt that the up-and-coming star would be a tremendous babe magnet for the series, drawing women viewers to CBS and driving ratings through the proverbial roof. Supposedly, Leonard was angered by what he perceived as a deliberate deception by Maharis about his sexuality, Leonard growing openly antagonistic towards him on the set. However, during a question and answer panel staged by The Paley Center For Media in 1990, both Leonard and Maharis sat next to one another, appearing quite cordial and enjoying a celebration of the series that they had created.

When Maharis developed hepatitis, and was confined to a hospital bed, Leonard assumed that it was merely a ploy by the actor to lobby for a raise in salary. For his part, Maharis had every reason to assume that when he returned to the show his workload would be lessened in deference to his recent sickness. Instead, the producer subjected him to grueling 15-hour workdays, often in sub-freezing temperatures. Leonard let it be known that he had a troublemaker and a prima donna on his hands and lost little time in spreading the word. He felt that the actor's sexual proclivities and continuing absences from the set had doomed his cash cow hit series. The producer had imagined taking the show, if not on the road then

"Even Stones Have Eyes" is George Maharis' favorite episode of the series. It deals with Buz becoming temporarily blinded by a construction accident.

Another publicity photo of Maharis and Milner posing in their Corvette with the Route 66 road sign featured predominantly in the background.

on the sea, with the travelers crossing the ocean to explore other countries in their signature Corvette. Maharis, on the other hand, was growing genuinely concerned for the state of his health, feeling that Leonard was irreparably hurting him. The actor grew increasingly resentful of his surroundings and position, eventually leaving the series for good.

With Herbert B Leonard spreading the word around the industry that Maharis was simply a negative influence who effectively murdered the future of his once popular series, the actor's reputation became irretrievably damaged. He found it increasingly difficult to find work worthy of his talents. Studios were afraid of his bad reputation. He did solid work as the lead in *The Satan Bug*, but starring roles became as elusive as the deadly infection of the film's title.

When Karen Funk Blocher finally interviewed Maharis in the early eighties, he was starring in summer stock and dinner theater. During the performance that Blocher witnessed, a particularly vitriolic elderly lady in a wheelchair was shockingly vocal about her own opinion of the actor's masculinity. It must have been a nightmare for Maharis who angrily defended his decision to leave *Route 66* for legitimate health concerns.

The roles eventually dried up entirely, and Maharis appeared on television as a supporting player on such shows as *Murder She Wrote* for the very network on which he'd once been a star. In more recent years, Maharis discovered another emerging talent as a sculptor and has become somewhat renowned as an artist, having his work as the focal point of numerous high-end shows at prestigious art galleries in and around San Francisco. For a time he also succeeded as a talented recording artist, recording two vocal albums and appearing as a guest on the weekly Judy Garland television series for CBS. Yet, his was an exciting and brilliant new talent that became tragically extinguished before its time ... a star blazing in the heavens, heartbreakingly obscured by clouds of jealousy and anger. I wished somehow that I could find and tell him just how deeply and profoundly his work impacted the lives of millions of fans ... particularly two brothers named Steve and Erwin, whose memories of Buz Murdock and Tod Stiles continued to shape and influence their world.

Fate would intervene, however, in the early hours of 2008. I had persuaded an acquaintance with personal contact information for Maharis to give me the address of either a publicist or advertising

The cash cow Corvette was seldom allowed to get this dirty in most episodes of *Route 66*.

Just watching this quick shot of George Maharis crossing the street conveys the gritty black-and-white photography and almost documentary realism the show projected.

representative. I wrote a short but passionate letter to him in which I spoke of my affection for his work, and of the profound influence that both the series and his character had had on my life. Some time had passed, and I had given up any hope of hearing from Maharis. I had been spending the last days of 2007 in San Francisco at the invitation of the legendary Castro Theater where I had programmed and co-hosted a nine-day Miklos Rozsa Festival, honoring the Oscar winning composer with 17 handpicked films. The composer's daughter, Juliet, had driven out from Los Angeles to join me on stage for an interview prior to a Saturday night screening of *Ben Hur*. Upon my return home to Philadelphia, I found a message awaiting me on my answer machine. It was from Maharis. The husky voice, although somewhat aged, was unmistakable. My eyes filled with tears as I listened to his words. He chuckled, mischievously I felt, as he briefly thanked me for my letter, sounding a trifle stunned, as he put it, that his performance had impacted my adolescence so profoundly. He said that he would attempt to contact me again when I might be home. I waited for that second telephone call to come. Sadly, he never called again.

Here's my final word concerning my affection for *Route 66* and its stars. The year was 1960, and I was reaching the end of my 13th year. The stodgy Eisenhower era was thankfully drawing to a close and my eyes were beginning to open to an awesome canvas of vibrant possibilities. I was becoming a man, and the responsibilities that lay ahead both thrilled and frightened me. I began to emerge cautiously from the protected haze of childhood, sensing an increasing awareness of what my impending maturity might offer. An air of excitement permeated the days and weeks that soon would dawn. Everything was new. Everyone was young.

Danny Ocean (in *Ocean's 11*) was rolling the dice in Vegas, while Frank Sinatra was re-inventing *cool*. Frank, Dean Martin and Sammy Davis, Jr. epitomized swinging and enthusiastic vitality. Their appetite for success, women and booze was hypnotic. A young, charismatic senator was charming the nation, and it wouldn't be long before John Fitzgerald Kennedy would ascend to political stardom and royalty as the youngest president in American history. Richard Burton was starring on Broadway as King Arthur in Lerner and Lowe's romantic fantasy, while young Kennedy would eventually have his political reign compared idealistically to the charmed and mythical kingdom of Camelot.

Tod and Buz became the wistful symbols of what the future might be holding for me as I prepared to lay the groundwork for leaving the safe, predictable confines of home and hearth, discovering success, adventure and romance on the road beneath their wheels. I was barely 14 years old, reveling in the sweeping winds of idealism blowing joyfully across America. These brave travelers seemed to encapsulate our dreams and yearnings as we lived vicariously through their weekly adventures. Within the fabled confines of that magical Corvette, the world was young once more, and so were we. A bright and shining optimism embraced America and there was, at long last, hope and promise for the future. *Route 66* signified for me the suggestion of "What dreams may come." Nothing was impossible, and the road awaited us. An endless panorama of limitless highways beckoned seductively. It was, perhaps, the most exciting period of my youth and innocence. Yet, I would never find my Shangri La. The journey ended prematurely ... on the crowded streets of Dallas as a series of bullets found their mark on November 22, 1963, shattering the euphoria of a kingdom not fully formed.

It all seems so long ago—a revered and precious dream eaten away by bitter years and tarnished experience. Where did it go? How could it have disappeared so quickly? I was an innocent, merely 13 years old, when I first joined Tod and Buz in the back seat of their handsome Corvette in 1960. Adolescence was a genuine promise, a tantalizing voyage mysteriously emerging from the shadows of childhood. Astonishingly, George and Marty are now in their eighth decade. I recently turned 66. I've undergone open-heart surgery, career displacement and divorce. And yet, in a strange way, *Route 66* symbolized the short-lived hope that tugged so longingly, once upon a time, at my young dreams and romantic aspirations. And so, for the wonder of that moment, forever frozen in time, its bittersweet road trip will ever occupy a deeply special place in my heart.

(*Route 66— The Complete Series* is now available on DVD, comprising 116 episodes on 24 discs, through Shout! Factory Home Entertainment.)

by Gary J. Svehla

Season One's Best in Crime and Suspense

In the 1980s, a local film club, one that I had inherited when the current president ran off to follow the love of his life and relocate in New Orleans, decided to change its name from The Count Dracula Society. The club wanted a name that captured a larger spectrum of the horror movie audience. One member, a young boy Ron, insisted we call the club The Thriller Society, mainly because Michael Jackson's *Thriller* was so hot at the moment and its iconic video nailed the current zombie-infested horror movie audience. If Ron had gone back another generation, he would have been reminded of Universal's *Thriller* anthology TV series, hosted by Boris Karloff from 1960-1962. Once again he may argue that the generic term "thriller" represented the entire spectrum of horror movies. However, even that series featured just as many crime, mystery and film noir-inspired entries as it featured full throttle horror chillers. In fact the series mostly covered stories that were not horrific in the monster or supernatural sense, but as host Karloff promised, "this is guaranteed to be a ... thriller!"

Image Entertainment released a box set of all 67 episodes of the series a few years back, many of them with audio commentary and some bonus features, including a preview promo for the series. We can once again evaluate the entirety of the series and not just the supernatural horror entries. I have decided to review the best non-horror entries here in *Mad About Movies* and the horror entries in our sister publication *Midnight Marquee*. As a child I only watched and remember the supernatural horror entries, as the other thriller-inspired entries did not interest me when I was 10 or 11 years old. But now as a dyed-in-the-wool thriller, suspense, mystery and film noir lover, these other entries are being viewed for, most likely, the very first time. This old set of eyes are able to evaluate a series that is now over 50 years old, yet vitally fresh and waiting for rediscovery. Taking my time and viewing each episode in order is a real kick, especially since I started watching the box set on the very night, 50 years later, when the very first episode premiered. Fifty years have gone by, but the series still generates tension and terror and the white-knuckle trip down memory lane has turned out to be a delightful one. My goal is not to review all the non-horror entries, but to select a handful of superior entries from season one and to express why and how they manage to hold up and remain meaningful cinema, half a century after the fact.

Merle Jenkins (George Grizzard) touches the cracked mirror representing his distorted view of reality in trying to become his boss Alan Patterson, from *The Twisted Image*.

The very first entry, *The Twisted Image*, directed by Arthur Hiller, adaptation by James P. Cavanagh, succeeds based upon the juxtaposition of two well-worn stereotypes. By presenting these two stereotypes in a clever manner concurrently, one pitted against the other, the stereotype becomes fresh. Business executive Alan Patterson (Leslie Nielsen) finds himself being stalked by new and lovely employee Lily (Natalie Trundy)—she with the haunting and bugged-out eyes—who wants to not only marry him, but to totally possess his every moment. Of course when she writes a letter to his wife Judy (Dianne Foster), the wife naturally suspects Alan of having an affair.

Alan Patterson (Leslie Nielsen) finds himself stalked by newly-hired employee Lily (Natalie Trundy), from *The Twisted Image*.

Boris Karloff introduces Mary Astor as Rose French, heavily made up, in the twisty *Rose's Last Summer*.

Meanwhile, equally psychotic newly-hired mail-room employee Merle Jenkins (an always excellent George Grizzard) wants to be Alan Patterson, even going as far as to steal his personal objects (his watch, for example) from his office desk. Things get interesting when Merle, almost believing he is Alan, makes a play for psycho-stalker Lily. Lily, of course, only has eyes for the real Alan and thinks the Merle substitute is third rate nerd all the way. Pretty soon, in the heat of passion, Merle strangles Lily to death and frames Alan for the crime.

I do not know what Alan Patterson's office manufactures or sells, but the firm certainly attracts the wrong type of people. Basically, the episode succeeds by nature of its three excellent performances, with Leslie Nielsen underplaying as the man who has to face the wrath of his angered wife and the suspicions of the police after people in the apartment building see Patterson leave Lily's room after she has been murdered. The screenplay goes over the top, but the taut direction of Arthur Hiller makes it all believable, and unlike *Alfred Hitchcock Presents*, the series upon which *Thriller* is based, the episode ends on a happy note.

Returning to the theme of people becoming someone they are not, *Rose's Last Summer* is another especially effective episode. Again directed by Arthur Hiller, with adaptation by Marie Baumer, silent screen star Mary Astor plays recovering boozing movie star Rose French. In the pre-titles sequence, Rose exits a tavern obviously drunk and stumbles into a truck that knocks her down and sends her to the hospital. Frank Clyde (Lin McCarthy) works with Rose at the rehabilitation hospital and becomes her friend. Rose is very anxious to announce she has accepted a new job that requires her to relocate, but she refuses to give any contact information. Rose vanishes but her gravesite is found eight days later in the garden of a large estate home, whose residents claim they do not know her. Curious that Rose supposedly died of heart failure when Rose recently had a physical and a clean bill of health, former husband Haley Dalloway (Jack Livesey) and Frank team up to speak to the people in the house where Rose died to find out the circumstances of her death. But the residents are all suspicious, nervous and refuse to speak.

The payoff arrives when we discover that the old bed-ridden lady of the house is not really the old lady of the house, but actually Rose made up to look just like the actual old woman. Rose was hired to impersonate the woman (now dead and buried) so her heirs would inherit money willed to them, but only after she reached 65 years of age. The problem is that after the conspirators receive their money, they don't need Rose to testify to the deceptive facts of the case, so in a wonderful conclusion, we have our greedy family members chase Rose down the dark, barren city streets trying to run her down in a speeding automobile. The car cuts across sidewalks and comes within inches of hitting the screaming, panicking impersonator, but she keeps a few feet ahead of her pursuers until Haley and Frank finally arrive on the scene to rescue her, a police car now in pursuit of the evil family members.

Once again Arthur Hiller's tense direction works in building suspense. Also successful is the manner in which the plot plays out, first with Rose's disappearance, then with her supposed death and aftermath. The viewer is constantly guessing what has happened to Rose and what is

***Thriller* often featured startling optical effects, such as this human skull superimposed over the head of Mary Astor from the beginning of *Rose's Last Summer*.**

Mob lawyer Lou Adams (Everett Sloane) gets a brow-beating from the powerful and ambitious Harry Gans (Jay C. Flippen), from *The Guilty Men*.

the secret of the family whose tranquil garden becomes the final resting place for … someone.

Perhaps the first true film noir episode, *The Guilty Men*, written by John Vlahos and directed by Jules Bricken, succeeds once again based upon its screenplay featuring conflicted moral ambiguity and strong performances. Punk kid Cesare Romano becomes syndicate boss Charlie Romano (Frank Silvera, looking and sounding very similar to a low-rent version of Marlon Brando's "Godfather," who is haunted by formerly ordering a gangland "hit" where innocent children were killed). Charlie, who has a loving wife Anna (Argentina Brunetti) but no children, wants the syndicate to go totally legit and back away from the importation of illegal drugs. His closest friend Lou Adams (the always wonderful Everett Sloane), the mob lawyer, is the wise and educated syndicate member who tends to agree with Charlie. However, ambitious and old school wannabe Harry Gans (Jay C. Flippen, still standing on both legs before his amputation occurred) wants the mob to vote Charlie out because he's soft. Also, Gans has papers in his safe deposit box that will incriminate Adams, so Adams is being strong-armed to vote with Gans against Charlie Romano. Charlie, who has difficulty getting the syndicate to approve a huge donation to a children's charity, has an impossible task convincing the boys to back off from drug trafficking. Charlie, who has a bad heart, succumbs to cinema's too oft used cliché, the sequence where he is having a heart attack and needs to reach for his pills, but the assembled few, including Gans and Lou Adams, stand by and watch him die. At his funeral Charlie's brother Tony, a respected doctor and one who loathes the mob, supports Charlie's wife Anna in refusing to accept the money the syndicate offers the family. Tony finally takes the donation after he sees that the money goes to charity, something Charlie would have wanted.

The noir aspect of moral ambiguity plays front and center, with the mob's dilemma to continue to kill innocent children by importing drugs into ghetto streets or make far less money, but legal money, by going totally legit in all business undertakings. Lou Adams is the man caught in the middle, the man who supports Charlie's morals but a man who is practical as well. The fact that he is being blackmailed only mucks up the already oily waters. But Lou tells his wife he will cooperate and spill the beans by talking to the feds, but he does not know his phone is being bugged by Gans and he and his boys are outside his home waiting for him. Lou is gunned down outside by machine gun blasts, but Gans does not get far, as the police are following his car

Everett Sloane as Lou, the mob mouthpiece, is fabulous; his debt to Charlie always comes first, as the mobster paid for Lou's law school expenses and set him up for life. However, as Charlie begins to flash a conscience, good friend Lou also begins to see the light and understands the mob can make more than enough money without the illegal activities. His guilt over allowing his friend to die a horrible, painful death only leads him to take action, spilling his guts to the federal authorities. Even though Lou dies

Charlie Romano (Frank Silvera), soon to be the former mob boss, suffers a fatal heart attack as his syndicate looks on and does nothing, from *The Guilty Men*.

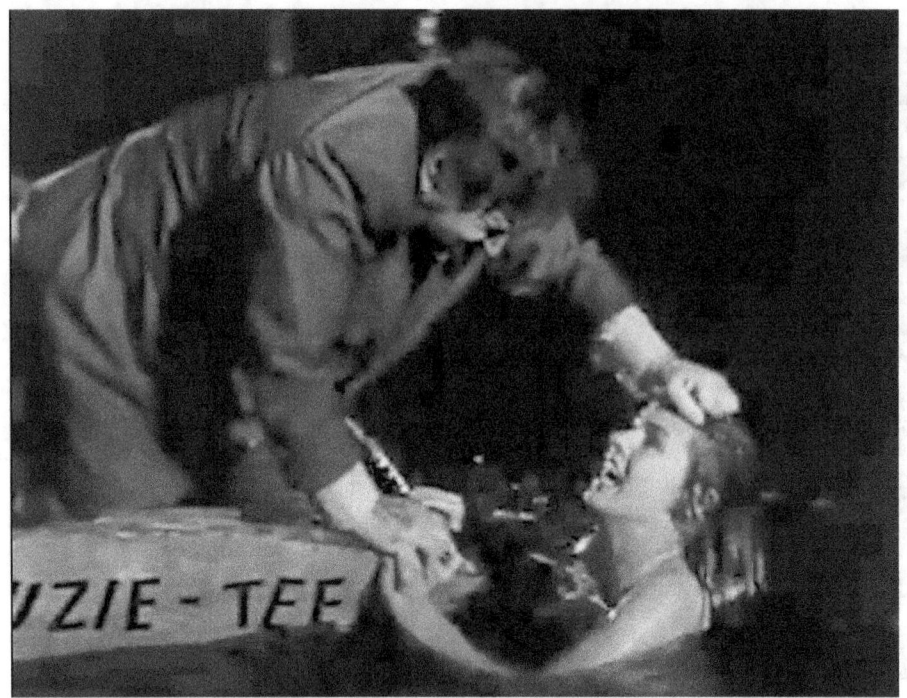

The savage Mr. Freitag (Martin Gabel) forces the head of the young girl underwater, drowning her, from the beginning of *The Watcher*.

in a hail of bullets, at least he dies knowing that finally, at last, he was doing the right thing. Television noir does not get better than this.

With the Halloween episode of season one, *The Purple Room*, William Frye debuted as the series' new producer and his emphasis focused a little more on supernatural horror and the gruesome. Another major change was the fact that Boris Karloff no longer wore or held his glasses during his intros. Without his specs, he did lend a more eerie figure to the proceedings. And strangely, after the *Psycho* house figured prominently in *The Purple Room* episode, it was the very next entry that featured *Thriller*'s take on Alfred Hitchcock's *Psycho*, released the same year. Instead of featuring the youthful and handsome psychotic killer that Anthony Perkins made iconic, *Thriller*'s take featured a more homely, squat, middle-aged Martin Gabel as the fiend, more akin to Robert Bloch's description of Norman Bates in his original novel. This suspenseful entry, entitled *The Watcher*, directed by horror film veteran John Brahm and scripted by Donald S. Sanford, begins and ends with two unnerving sequences. In the initial pitch-black beginning, we see fiend Mr. Freitag (Gabel) in a rowboat docked at a pier. He uses all his strength to push a beautiful and struggling young girl underwater. She soon succumbs and drowns, while Freitag stares at his scratched hands. For network television in 1960, I could not think of a more unnerving beginning.

It seems that Freitag is a high school teacher who spends his summers in Lakeside, a folksy resort community. A strange little man who always seems to be wearing suits, ties and hats, he even comforts the grieving mother of the young girl he killed at the dock. But he becomes the watcher, a man who becomes obsessed when handsome young man Larry (Richard Chamberlain) seems to have more than kisses on his mind when dating young socialite Bess (Olive Sturgess). When healthy 20-somethings seem to be flirting with sex, Freitag sees himself as the moral cleanser of society. Of course Larry's aunt (widowed, thus forcing Larry to become the man of the house) hates Bess, and Bess' uptight mother hates the lowly Larry, even though Bess' alcoholic uncle supports her romance.

While Larry and Bess are on a picnic excursion in the woods, in rapid fire succession Bess sprains her ankle and Larry finds his car has a flat tire. Leaving Bess alone and locked safely in the car, he thumbs a ride to town, with the tire, to have it repaired. However, Freitag, the perverse watcher, sneaks on his hands and knees around the side of the car and suddenly tries to rip the car door open. Instead, he rips the metal handle off the frame and uses it to attempt to break the glass and attack screaming Bess. Wisely, the girl honks her horn, which Freitag dismantles. He flees as Bess passes out. Meanwhile, Freitag follows Larry to the service station fixing the tire. Sneaking up from behind, Freitag clunks him over the head with a wrench and lowers the auto lift as we cut to commercial, the implica-

Martin Gabel's intense gaze from behind window curtains reveals the true evil character that lies beneath the surface, from *The Watcher*.

tion being that Larry will soon be crushed to death if he survived the bump on the head.

In the final act, Larry is groggy but will recover and Bess goes to nurse him, against her mother's wishes. Left alone up in the bedroom, Freitag sneaks up behind Bess and attempts to push her against the wall, but she responds by smashing a water vase against his head, opening a bloody wound. In the episode's only awkward moment, we hear but do not see Freitag fall through a second story bedroom window, landing on the lawn below in a heap of mangled gore. The episode ends quite spectacularly as we watch Bess' face stare out the window and scream bloody murder.

The Watcher is superb and comes close to being a horror entry, but I believe its criminal psycho-killer focus makes it more a crime entry. The direction is always gripping with shots of the bland killer appearing in darkened doorways, never saying a word until someone discovers his presence. Many early scenes, such as Freitag walking out of the boarding house, are made spooky because a sudden clash of thunder booms forth or soaking rain suddenly appears. Martin Gable submits a stellar performance by mostly underplaying his fiendish role and presenting the banality of horror in the guise of a teacher, a mild man that most everyone ignores. Most of the episode is photographed in shadows and at nighttime and the goose bumps keep rising throughout. *The Watcher* is a wonderful episode of the series and its similarities to *Psycho* are very interesting.

Lt. Rome (Robert Lansing) grabs the purse of Jane Kimball (Whitney Blake), as Sgt. Dumont (Steve Brodie) looks on, from *The Fatal Impulse*.

The Fatal Impulse, directed by Gerald Mayer from a screenplay by Philip MacDonald, is simply an exciting thriller with involving characters. The setup is gripping. A limping and disheartened Harry Elser (the always wonderful Elisha Cook, Jr.) is unhappy that big city politico Walker Wylie (Conrad Nagel) is running for mayor. While attempting to plant a small explosive device in Wylie's office desk before a major TV interview program, Elser is caught by a secretary and flees to the elevator to escape. However, while in the crowded shaft, he plants his home-made bomb into the pocket or purse of one of the women occupying the elevator. Of course the audience does not see who gets the hot potato, and the rest of the hour is filled with dedicated cops Lt. Rome (Robert Lansing) and Sgt. Dumont (Steve Brodie) attempting to identify and locate all the elevator occupants, to check their purses and save their lives. Rome is a sad figure, having been widowed several years ago and now burying his pain by living only for his job. Buddy Dumont, who lost a young child and recently had another with his wife, claims that Rome might still find the love of his life if he simply allows himself the chance to create a new life outside the office.

Artist Jane Kimball (Whitney Blake), who spends too much time in a seedy bar restaurant with a cocktail-wielding date, is questioned in a suspenseful sequence that requires Rome to carry Kimball's purse gingerly outside as she glances through the nearby window at his actions. When the bomb is not found, Kimball, who was present in the elevator, offers to sketch the faces of the other passengers that she remembers. As the hour continues, one thing or another leads Rome back to see Kimball, either at the restaurant or at her home. Kimball is immediately attracted to Rome and admires his steely courage

This studio-created film noir shadow-dominated street corner from *The Fatal Impulse* demonstrates just how effective the sets created for *Thriller* actually were.

Ruth (Beverly Garland) holds up a copy of the newspaper detailing the crimes of the Silk Stocking Strangler, from *Knock Three-One-Two*.

and determination, and pretty soon her current beau is cut loose as Rome and her are drawn closer together. Sadly, in another exciting sequence, as the police descend upon Elser's home and garage, the likable Sgt. Dumont is blown to smithereens by a booby-trapped explosive.

As Rome and his team methodically eliminate every person on the elevator, realizing that the bomb is set to detonate at 11 p.m., they are frustrated. Of course, it turns out that the bomb was not in Jane Kimball's purse, but rather in her art portfolio, which her mother moved when she arrived home, allowing the small bomb to fall out and become embedded beneath a sofa pillow. In one of the return visits to interview Kimball, the clock ticks closer to 11 p.m. as the little package lies undetected.

It is rare when taut, suspenseful direction combines with interesting characters to produce a one-two punch. In this episode *Thriller* demonstrates why its non-supernatural horror episodes are often the equal of the ghastly horror episodes. Sometimes these episodes resemble *Alfred Hitchcock Presents*, but such a comparison is only a tribute to the quality produced by *Thriller*, week after week.

Knock Three-One-Two was another surprising and pretty effective episode. Directed by Herman Hoffman from a script by John Kneubuhl, *Knock Three-One-Two* features a solid performance by Joe Maross as Ray Kenton, a sorry loser, whose job as liquor salesman draws him into backrooms of bars, resulting in huge gambling losses. Because of his pathetic nature, he is able to convince the mobsters to give him another day to repay his $1500 debt, but in order to get extra time, he now owes double the amount. His wife Ruth, a lovely Beverly Garland, has been depleting her savings account to pay off Ray's debts, but she has decided to finally hold the line. No more money! In the meanwhile a serial killer of women, the Silk Stocking Strangler, terrifies the city, and by chance, Ray can identify the killer when he sees the fiend escaping from a murder scene. Imagine Ray's surprise when the killer turns up at a bar he frequents. Ray concocts a plan to set up his wife's murder with his purposeful too loose mouth whereby he reveals to the killer his home address and his secret knock (three knocks, one knock, two knocks). Ray even creates an alibi by having his developmentally challenged (and guilt ridden) friend Benny (a young Warren Oates), who has confessed to the police for the murders several times in the past but never been taken seriously, phone him at the bar and call him down to headquarters, just when the actual murder of his wife occurs. Ray cannot be accused of the crime in such a scenario and can inherit his wife's money, since she no longer intended to bankroll his gambling debt.

In an exciting finale, we observe as the Silk Stocking Strangler gains access to Ruth's apartment and he overpowers her. But just as the strangler produces the trademark silk stocking from his pocket, Ruth's boss and friend, who just dropped her off, senses something is wrong, so he turns his car around and races back to the apartment. But will he arrive in time?

Basically, Joe Maross creates a multi-dimensional portrait of a man caught in the middle between his love for his wife and the fear for his own life. Ray Kenton is a sleaze, a loser and a user, but the audience still feels sorrow for him. How-

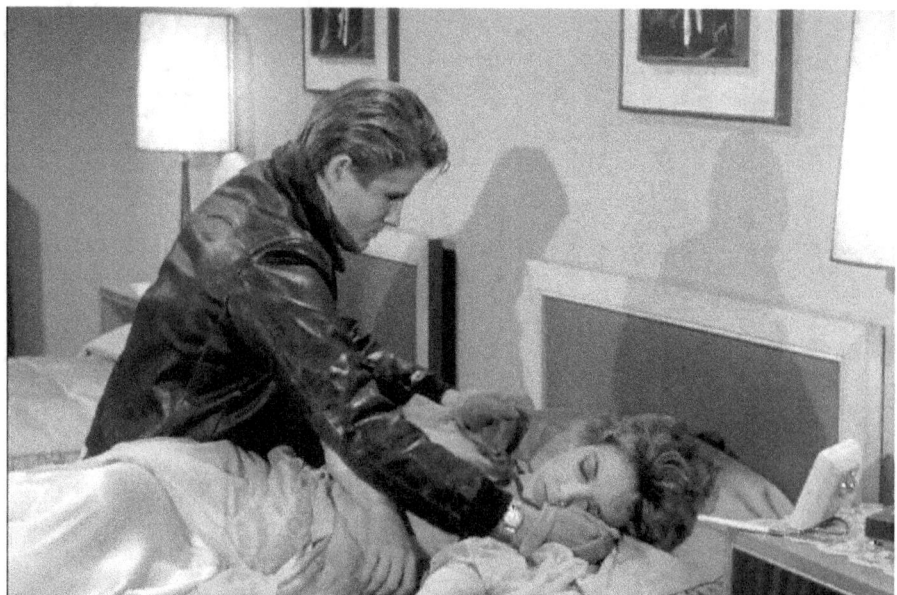

The Silk Stocking Strangler (Meade Martin) is about to claim another victim, Ruth, moments before her boss breaks into the apartment to save her, from *Knock Three-One-Two*.

The good news is that the locksmith got the trunk open; the bad news is that a dead body is found inside the trunk, from *The Merriweather File*.

ever, after he concocts the scheme to use a serial killer to kill his wife for her life's saving, justice is served in the very final minutes. Irony runs rampant in this excellent *Thriller* episode, where the clever script combines with insightful characterizations and suspenseful direction to produce a superb thriller.

The Merriweather File, directed by horror specialist John Braham from the novel by Lionel White (and screenplay by John Kneubuhl), is both edge-of-the-seat suspenseful and yet features a twisty, complex plot that keeps the audience guessing, right up until the end. Like a game of cat-and-mouse, the episode's revelation comes in the final seconds of the story, told against the background of trimming a Christmas tree.

The episode begins with a black-cloaked murderer inside a suburban home. The silent fiend seals the back door with a towel and plugs the broken glass panel where he gained access to the house, as he turns on the kitchen range's gas jets, attempting to murder Ann Merriweather (Bethel Leslie) while she sleeps. However the house cat overturns a metal tray and awakens her and she rushes next door to seek comfort in the arms of family friend and lawyer Howard Yates (James Gregory). It seems that Ann has attempted suicide in the past, suffering extreme guilt over accidentally running over and killing her only child in the family driveway. Even though she and husband Charles (Ross Elliott) seem to be the perfect couple, their child's death has created a chasm in their perfect relationship. Distraught wife Ann has a horrible headache as a result of the break in and murder attempt and tells Charles to go to the club and have some drinks with the boys, even though he specifically returned from the road (he is a traveling salesman) to spend time with Ann for their wedding anniversary. Charles secretly blames his wife for their child's death and keeps a woman on the side, Virginia Grant (K.T. Stevens). Returning home from a night of drinking and passion, Charles has a flat tire and is stranded on the side of the road (he lost his trunk key). Waving down the police, the police tell him they will get help for him and pretty soon a locksmith from the repair shop gets the trunk open, but unfortunately a dead man is curled up inside the trunk and Charles is booked for murder. Charles uses his neighbor Howard for legal council and tells Howard his alibi was spending the night with his lover, Virginia, but he does not wish to reveal that fact, as he doesn't wish to harm his wife's already fragile psyche.

Before long the murderer-in-black returns one more time to the Merriweather home for another attack. Charles' pistol (the same one used to kill the dead man in the trunk) is found in the garbage can out back and the story becomes more complex as the hour speeds along. Before long Charles is even doubted by friend Howard and, at the trial, Charles is convicted and eventually executed. In the story's quiet Christmastime epilogue, a police detective visits the house to tell Charles the convoluted truth of the case, that Ann was the murderer and that she cold-bloodedly planned her revenge to make Charles suffer for his marital indiscretions. However, as the story is about to close, Howard places tinsel on the tree as Ann returns home with presents in hand, Howard introducing Ann as his wife to the startled police detective. The glum, desperate look on Howard's face says it all, as the story ends.

What makes *The Merriweather File* so exceptional is the intensity that exists between well-drawn characters in a very small cast. We have the beautiful but often hysterical wife Ann, who is forced to live mostly alone in a very big and dark house. Howard Yates is the decent next-door neighbor, who has passion bubbling underneath the surface for his good friend's wife, but out of respect for friend Charles, he never acts upon his physical attraction, at least while Charles is alive. Somewhat dorky and balding, Charles is a man too quick to break out into laughter and caught in too many lies to be entirely trustworthy. And the relationships between these three intensify making twists and turns as the audience attempts to figure out who is the dead man in the trunk and why was he killed ... and by whom? Again, in the best tradition of *Thriller*, this episode is jam-packed with tension and a twisting plot that keeps us guessing until the end.

A rather flawed episode, *Last Date*, contains some inspiring moments of tension. Based upon a Cornell Woolrich story adapted by Donald S. Sanford, *Last Date* demonstrates that director Herschel Daugherty knows how to generate slow-building tension. First the flaws, just to get them out of the way. The stars are Larry Pennell as Larry Weeks, brother to James Weeks, played by Edward Platt, just a few years before he drew attention for playing "Chief" on TV's *Get Smart*. Pennell plays the younger brother who wears a tight fitting tee and pompadour, while graying and balding Platt seems more like a father figure than a brother. Secondly, the convoluted plot just tries a little too hard to set up the delicate situations. The story starts off as the older James, who

Charles (Ross Elliott) and wife Ann Merriweather (Bethel Leslie) in happier times in *The Merriweather File*

Stepdaughter Helen's (Jody Fair) leg is only inches away from discovering the dead body, from *Last Date*.

suddenly appears at the beach house, strangles his over-sexed wife. Overcome with guilt, James leaves the beautiful corpse sprawled all over the bed, and he plans to turn himself into the police. However beefcake brother Larry figures out the perfect foolproof plan and alibi for his older brother. It involves the fact that James did not use his commuter ticket the morning of the murder, leaving it at home. So unless anyone recognizes him, no one could prove he visited the seaside resort the day of the murder. Larry wants James to ride home and go out with the boys drinking, and later that night he will phone with the bad news and James can act surprised, shocked and grief-stricken. In the meanwhile, Larry will dispose of the body.

Here is where the story takes off. As Larry waits until sunset to clear out the body, he has to make sure nobody comes into her bedroom, and just who happens to appear but stepdaughter Helen, who has to change from her revealing swimsuit into something presentable for her evening date. And it seems the bathroom has adjoining doors to enter either bedroom, hers and her mother's. And she wants to use some of her mother's things to better impress her date. So when she is in the bathroom, the mother's bedroom door is ajar, with Larry hiding in the shadows. He manages to move the corpse to the side of the bed, away from the bathroom, where he slumps down and hides as Helen sneaks into the darkened room and admires herself in the full-length mirror. As she backs away from the mirror, we see one lower leg and foot extend from the side of the bed, and Helen comes inches away from brushing against the corpse. The sequence is edited and photographed for maximum suspense.

When Larry prepares to carry out and deposit the corpse in the trunk of his car, he first spots a busy-body neighbor who watches everything while sitting in her rocker on the porch, so Larry decides to hide the corpse by rolling it up in a large throw rug, stuffing pillows in each end to make sure shoes and other stuff do not fall out. Being a body-builder type, he easily carries the stiff carpet on his shoulder and out the door. He clears out the trunk of his car, including the spare tire, to stuff the body inside.

One of the dead woman's lovers phones and wants to meet the woman that night, and fast thinking Larry tells him she got tied up but that she would meet him at 8:30 at a local nightspot, that he should park on the outskirts of the parking lot. Larry plans to dump the corpse into this sap's car and let him do all the explaining.

Of course Larry is speeding around sharp curves and corners and flattens his tire, and now without a spare tire, he has to walk a few miles with the carpet/corpse atop his shoulders. When a suspicious truck driver offers him a ride and Larry accepts, the driver speeds up the vehicle and pushes Larry out onto the side of the road, where he also throws the carpet and corpse. Unconscious but quickly reviving, Larry resumes carrying the body, even though it is now a few minutes past 8:30. But Larry sees his patsy who impatiently goes inside the club to check on his date, and this provides Larry ample time to unroll the rug and throw the corpse into the back seat of the convertible.

Unknown to Larry, who hurries home to find his guilty brother waiting there for him, the now drunk sucker on the parking lot speeds off down the highway thinking his date stood him up. He soon wrecks the car killing himself. The police arrive at Larry's home to inform James that his wife was killed in an automobile crash, thus clearing him of any illegal activity. But as soon as the police

Larry (Larry Pennell) is watching the patsy who will go inside looking for his date so the corpse can be placed in the car's backseat, from *Last Date*.

leave, James still announces his intention of confessing everything to the police. In an almost comical aside, Larry bellows under his breath, "All this for nothing," as we remember all the close calls and the corpse-carrying marathon that Larry has undergone to protect his brother. But as the episode ends James dutifully marches out to the still parked police car, ending the episode on a rather ironic note.

The sequences of young Helen in her stepmother's bedroom, inches away from seeing her cold corpse, and the tense shots of sneaking the corpse out of the house hidden in a rug, the car breaking down and Larry lugging that dead weight for many more miles only amps up the suspense. The irony of having the wife's lover wreck his car and *killing* the woman is very ironic, but when James reveals he will still confess for the crime takes the wind out of Larry's sails (who now can be held as an accomplice to murder). While the story adaptation is flawed, the individual suspense sequences are true nail-biters and hold our attention for the hour.

Rumor has it that Alfred Hitchcock, feeling threatened by the similarities between his series *Alfred Hitchcock Presents* and *Thriller* (both Universal productions), was the major reason why the series was canceled after just two seasons. In another episode from season one, *A Good Imagination*, *Thriller* creates that ironic, semi-humorous crime thriller that the Hitchcock series did so well. This *Thriller* seems as though it could have been produced for the Hitchcock series. *A Good Imagination* is atypical of *Thriller*, containing far more humor and irony than the series displayed, up until this point. Directed by John Brahm from a screenplay by Robert Bloch, based upon his own story, the episode becomes a showcase for actor Edward Andrews, who performs expertly as Frank Logan, bookworm, murderer and man of vivid imagination.

The story is deceptively simple but it is the tone of irony and cozy mystery that makes this episode exceptional. And without the *tour-de-force* performance by Andrews, the show would fall flat. The episode's success belongs mainly to him.

Frank Logan is a bookstore owner, past middle age, well dressed but conservatively, moon-faced and pudgy, a man

Bookish Frank Logan (Edward Andrews), posing with his wife Louise (Patricia Barry), steals the show in *A Good Imagination*.

who wears thick horn-rimmed glasses. He's well spoken, totally non-threatening and what we would call nerdish. Ah, but his wife Louise (Patricia Barry), middle-aged, attractive, but in a classy sense, has been having affairs when Frank is away at book conventions or trapped running his shop. The episode starts as Louise's lover Randy, a quite dapper man who rents a luxury apartment, is awakened in the middle of the night, arises, and finds his apartment ransacked. Sitting quietly in a chair, reading a copy of *War and Peace*, is milquetoast Frank. Frank reveals he knows about the affair he and his wife are having, Frank having found the key to Randy's apartment in Louise's possession. Using a weapon from the Middle Ages that hangs on the wall, Frank murders Randy, making it appear that robbery was the motive.

After Louise returns from Randy's funeral, a man she confesses to Frank she hardly knew, Frank produces the key to Randy's apartment and hands the key to Louise, thus allowing her to realize he knows everything and that Randy's murder was most likely a product of Frank's ingenuity. Louise goes to her brother and tells him about her affair and he in turn hires a private investigator to connect the dots, tying Frank to the murder. The investigator Joe Thorp (Ken Lynch) does exactly that, but he first goes to Frank and states, for $10,000, he will tell the brother that he found nothing. The deal will be sealed at a fishing cabin tomorrow night where Thorp will appear an hour before

Frank Logan with George Parker (Ed Nelson), both a handyman and his wife's lover, from *A Good Imagination*.

the brother is to arrive. However, Frank is already there, wearing silly looking fishing gear and a cap with sharp lures. Of course Thorp has already been disposed of and the brother shares a drink with Frank before learning that Thorp is dead, his corpse sitting upright in a rowboat in back. Of course Frank gives the brother a drink from the same bottle and he is soon dead, or at least unconscious, and both men are taken to the middle of the lake where the boat is overturned, making it appear each died from a fishing accident. Quietly afterwards Frank is again reading a book, this time *An American Tragedy*.

In the final act Frank buys a summer place to allow Louise to recover from the two deaths. She will stay alone during the week and Frank will join her during the weekends, when he can get away. However, handsome and amorous handyman George Parker (hunky Ed Nelson) makes his services available to Louise and they instantly lock lips and begin necking on the coach. Of course Frank catches on quite rapidly that his wife is having another fling and he puts into action a plan to dispatch both of them. Using Poe's *The Black Cat* as inspiration, Frank has George patch up a large hole in his basement, only afterwards telling him Louise is bound and tied and suffocating behind the newly erected brick wall that he has constructed. George leaves, planning to run to the police, but Louise, driving home, is stopped by the police, who can confirm that she is alive and well and that George is a ranting and raving lunatic. Frank, having sold the house, plans to leave the next morning, already having established his alibi that Louise was seen alive. Of course that evening when Louise comes home, Frank actually does murder his wife by sealing her in the walled up space that he already knocked back down.

But Frank's plans are foiled when the sheriff orders his deputies to take the arrested George back to Frank's place so he can see that Louise is alive and this truth will snap George back to reality and wellness. But the look on Frank's face says it all, knowing he has trapped himself when he actually buried his wife's body in the cemented and patched up hole in the wall. With a repeated nervous laugh, the episode fades to its end credits.

Again, such subtle irony is more common to *Alfred Hitchcock Presents*, but *Thriller* does a fantastic job making this episode shine based upon a taut script filled with twists and surprises, marvelous performances (chiefly Edward Andrews) and exciting direction by veteran John Brahm. Just having Frank read specific novels that comment upon the crime he just committed sparks a smile on the viewers' lips again and again. This may be an odd episode but it is a memorable one that continues to hold up well.

Season one of *Thriller* offered 37 episodes comprising crime, mystery, suspense and supernatural horror. Out of the 37 episodes of season one, we have covered 9 superior non-horror episodes, or roughly one-quarter of season one. While *Thriller* has gained the reputation of being the best horror anthology series ever produced, we can see (by the series title alone) that the success of the so-called sidebar horror episodes, beginning with *The Purple Room*, pushed the series to explore more supernatural horror and fewer crime, mystery and suspense stories as the series found its creative footing. But hopefully it can be shown that the non-horror episodes often sparkled just as brightly as the classic horror ones. So many superior non-horror episodes are forgotten or seldom seen to this day and are ripe for rediscovery. For a TV series called *Thriller*, would we want it any other way?

Edward Andrews' eyes can instantly flip from bland to insane in a moment.

The Warner Archive Collection has made available as two of their "Made to Order" DVDs the 1933 Paramount drama *One Sunday Afternoon*, as well as its 1941 Warner Brothers remake, *The Strawberry Blonde,* with James Cagney. One might think a MOD release is a surprisingly shabby treatment for a much-loved Hollywood classic like *The Strawberry Blonde*, but in making both versions available, it finally allows anyone with access to the New York City library system the enviable opportunity to compare both movies with the script of the original 1933 Broadway stage play, "One Sunday Afternoon" by James Hagan.

Back in the teens and twenties James Hagan was a working stiff Broadway stage actor who turned to writing with the Broadway productions of "Guns" in 1928 and "Mid-West" in 1936. Neither play was particularly successful, running 48 and 22 performances respectively, nor neither has ever been revived on Broadway or adapted for film or television. Hagan appears to have given up acting with "Guns," and he does not have any credits as either actor or writer in films. Hagan's last professional credit, a mere two years after having his name on the marquee of "Mid-West," is as stage manager for the Broadway production of "Here Come the Clowns" by Philip Barry. He died in 1947, and not in New York.

But before then, Hagan left one big ripple in the show business sea with "One Sunday Afternoon." In addition to its respectable nine-month Broadway run and the two films covered here, Raoul Walsh directed a musical adaptation, also titled *One Sunday Afternoon*, in 1949. In the Golden Age of television drama (1949-1959), the play was adapted for television no less than six times.

"One Sunday Afternoon" first opened on February 15, 1933 and closed in November 1933, while the movie premiered on the first of September the same year. Not only is that an incredibly short time for a property to make the jump from the Great White Way to Hollywood, it means that the movie opened while the Broadway cast (headed by Lloyd Nolan) was still performing. That is very unusual, since most plays were contracted to prevent a movie's premier until after the Broadway run has ended (*Arsenic and Old Lace* had to wait almost three *years* from completion to final release). Maybe Paramount was one of the original investors and set the terms of the contract. And maybe Hagan didn't have a choice.

The play opens with a prologue set in the present day (1933). Biff, an unsuccessful dentist married to Amy,

holds a grudge against Hugo, who stole Biff's girl Virginia. By chance Hugo comes to Biff's office to have a tooth pulled. To relieve the pain, Biff hooks Hugo up to a gas inhaler, with the intention of letting Hugo suffocate under the gas. As Hugo goes under, the scene shifts to:

Act I: "Some years earlier" Biff is a working class laborer who dreams of becoming a dentist. Everyone thinks Biff is a bully because he is always getting into fights, but the play makes clear that his reputation is unjust, as he is usually sticking up for someone weaker than himself. Biff is sweet on Virginia, who doesn't trust Biff due to his reputation for violence. She is more interested in Hugo, who slowly steals Virginia out from under Biff's nose. Virginia has a friend, Amy, who has been sweet on Biff since they were kids, but Biff never noticed her. Okay, that's the set-up. When Biff

Right to left: Biff (Gary Cooper) single-mindedly eyes his object of desire, Virginia (Fay Wray), as the girl who really loves him, Amy (Frances Fuller), looks on. False friend Hugo (Neil Hamilton) adds his greedy glare.

gets into too many fights, Hugo sees his chance and elopes with Virginia. Brokenhearted, Biff starts spending time with Amy.

Act II: Three years later, Biff is married to Amy, but still longs for Virginia. Hugo has become a big shot at the factory where Biff works (six months away from becoming a dentist). Hugo still harbors a long-simmering jealousy towards Biff, has Biff fired and Biff flies off the handle and ends up in jail. Two years later, Biff returns from jail and pledges himself to Amy.

The play ends in an epilogue, picking up where the prologue left off. As Hugo goes under from the gas, Virginia enters. As the stage directions make clear: "She has become a coarse type of person, a washed-out blonde, extravagantly dressed." In other words, she has turned into a complete floozy, who now seems to like Biff and would not be too sad if Hugo dies under the gas. Biff comes to his senses, sends Hugo and Virginia on their way and has a final reconciliation with Amy, who of course was always the girl for him.

One Sunday Afternoon is practically a scene-by-scene, line-by-line adaptation of the play "One Sunday Afternoon." In the movie Gary Cooper plays Biff, Fay Wray is Virginia, and Frances Fuller is Amy. Much of the dialogue has been edited out to reduce the film to a merciful 69 minutes, but this is one of those completely stage-bound early talkies where there is no musical score and has a pace described by my gal Judi as "glacial." The script does not play to Gary Cooper's strengths, giving him much more dialogue than he is comfortable with, and Cooper's slow-to-anger delivery slows the movie down so it feels twice the length. Unfortunately, lost in the cuts are all the references to Biff being a defender of the weak, so much so no reason exists for us to believe that Biff is anything but the bully everybody thinks he is. The moments when Biff starts to warm up to Amy are also lost. Instead, Biff impulsively weds Amy on the same night that Hugo runs off with Virginia, just so that none of their friends will think that Hugo has put anything over on him. This makes Biff look like he's rather callously using Amy's very real love for him. So much is cut out that almost no tenderness exists between Biff

James Cagney as Biff and Rita Hayworth as Virginia

and Amy, not until the moment when Biff comes home after spending two years in prison for assault. In both play and movie they meet in the park. In the play, Biff has several pages of dialogue about the moon, the stars, the rain, etc. before walking off with Amy. The movie cuts all of this and simply has Biff fall to his knees and lay his head in Amy's lap. It is the best moment in the whole affection-starved movie. Frances Fuller does great work as Amy, really making us believe that she would actually love this brute. Fay Wray is fine as Virginia, and given how superior she acts toward Biff, it is fun to see her turn slutty in the last scene.

Warner Brothers remade the script after only eight years. Unbelievable. And made it a major studio release.

The Strawberry Blonde is a total re-imaging of "One Sunday Afternoon." Screenwriters Julius and Philip Epstein add depth to the plot, to the characters, to the historical background, to every aspect of the film. Most importantly the Epsteins and director Raoul Walsh raise the Gay Nineties nostalgia already present in the stage play to operatic heights. Scenes of poverty that had real Depression-era desperation in the first film are here given a sepia coloring—by the soundtrack of sweet old songs whose words seem to be part of our very DNA, the straw hats, the German beer gardens, the bars serving a free lunch, a Harlem that is mostly forest, all the way to the film's concluding sing-a-long of "And the Band Played On" done in the style of old Nickelodeon slide projections.

The film takes its sweet time getting started, spending a full 20-minutes just to introduce all the characters, including an extended scene with Alan Hale as Biff's Dad who wasn't even in the original play. *The Strawberry Blonde* is a whole half hour longer than the first film, but it doesn't seem half the length.

Biff is no longer a brute, his bad reputation is due entirely to his father, whom Alan Hale makes a lovable old tippler. Biff's adversary Hugo (Jack Carson) becomes a downright bad guy who makes his fortune from out-and-out fraud. When Biff goes to jail, it is not because of his own violent temper, as in the play and first film, but because he is the fall guy in one of Hugo's frauds.

This is James Cagney's film and Cagney is, well, Cagney. He brings bottomless depth of feeling to the character of Biff, with that Cagney mix of vulnerability and two-fisted charisma that makes him lovable even when he is threatening to punch out George Reeves.

With a little help from the Epsteins, Rita Hayworth makes the perfect Virginia, the girl all men fall for without ever knowing who she really is. While

While *The Strawberry Blonde* remains Cagney's film, Rita Hayworth's Virginia becomes the quintessential fun date.

a little jaded in the final scene, she does not become the floozy Fay Wray became in the first film. In her earlier scenes, Wray's Virginia could not wait for the opportunity to dump Cooper's Biff, but Hayworth's Virginia is the quintessential fun date. While Biff courts her, she is never haughty or distant, but carries a pleasant, open sense of fun and self-entitlement that, while undeniably attractive, few men could actually satisfy. Audiences understand Biff's attraction, while still being glad he doesn't win her.

For those of us who grew up watching *The Adventures of Superman,* there is something touching about seeing George Reeves, in his minor role as a college boy, thoroughly enjoying his big moment in the Hollywood spotlight.

For my money, though, the real stand-out performance is by Olivia De Havilland as Amy. She is helped enormously by the unusual depth given her character by the Epsteins' script, which among other things makes her much less of a doormat. She is charming and funny in her early scenes as a young freethinker, and the scene where she shocks the young Biff with a knowing wink that actually knows a lot less than it lets on is delightful. Unlike the original play, her Amy does not start out the film in love with Biff, and De Havilland takes us through every step of her relationship with Biff, from their early banter and tentative rapport, to the casual intimacy of young married life, to the stirrings of marital discontent, all the while she remains the woman any working man would want to come home to. Unfortunately, De Havilland is much too pretty to be believable as Rita Hayworth's plain-Jane girlfriend.

With its easy-going nostalgia and the sugar-coating that makes even Biff's three-year jail sentence look easy, I'm sure that the Elia Kazans and Marlon Brandos who would soon bring naked emotion and documentary realism to Hollywood films thought *The Strawberry Blonde* was a piece of enjoyable trash. But as a product of the Hollywood dream factory at its zenith, with a creative cast and crew working at the height of their powers, the film, while never particularly realistic, achieves the heightened emotion of opera. Perhaps *One Sunday Afternoon* actually comes closer to the facts of early 20th-Century life, but the world of *The Strawberry Blonde* is the one you wish were true. As a piece of American mythology, it is perfect.

My special thanks go out to Anthony Ambrogio for his help with this article.

MAD ABOUT MOVIES BOOK REVIEW

BY GARY J. SVEHLA

Mystery Movie Series of 1940s Hollywood by Ron Backer; McFarland www.mcfarlandpub.com; Order 800-253-2187; 322 pages soft cover $45

One of the thrills of being an avid movie buff is discovering new treasures. For me the past few years have been exciting discovering many of the B-movie mystery series that Hollywood churned out during the decade of the 1940s. As a child I was aware of famous 1930s mystery series such as *Charlie Chan, Mr. Motto* and *The Thin Man*. But when it came to the equally entertaining but lesser known series, *The Falcon* was perhaps the only series of which I was aware. But most of these other series were not regularly shown on television. In recent years Turner Classic Movies began screening most of the 1940s mystery series, many of them based upon pulp detective fiction or popular radio series of their day. After becoming acquainted with *Boston Blackie, The Lone Wolf, Michael Shayne, The Whistler, The Crime Doctor, The Falcon, Ellery Queen* and *The Shadow* (to name most but not all of the series), I was especially delighted to discover that Ron Backer did a two-volume book series detailing the American mystery movie series of both the 1930s and the 1940s. Besides watching and enjoying these programmers, fans could now read up about the origins and development of each series, with detailed production background included.

Besides the mystery series mentioned above, Backer also covers *The Saint, Sherlock Holmes, Nick Carter, Mr. District Attorney, Wally Benton*, the Universal *Inner Sanctum* series, *Dick Tracy, Philip Marlowe* (not actually a B-series and for me out of place with the other series covered) and a few others.

Backer does an excellent job with each of the series analyzed. He usually

starts out by covering the literary roots if the lead character first appeared on the printed page. Often name changes occurred with the transformation from printed page to radio to the movies and Backer addresses such changes (name changes occurred with *The Crime Doctor* and *The Falcon* heroes, among others). Usually a radio series followed from the pulp fiction, and Backer seems to enjoy differentiating the changes that occurred in the translation from radio to the silver screen. And finally, Backer covers each entry in each mystery series in detail, comparing the merits of each film to all the others. Even among B-productions, some films rise up while others sink, and Backer lets us know exactly why. Each movie typically contains a long synopsis, not necessarily a flaw because most of these movies have been difficult to find until recently. However, for my taste, Backer does not spend quite enough space devoted to a critical analysis of each film, even though he does critique every film. I wish the space devoted to synopsis and analysis had been better balanced. Backer knows his stuff and I wanted to hear more of his personal opinions. When reviewing a series, for instance, he notes those entries where the director does a good job or bad job, and why. He notes which entry becomes a true film noir and which entries use archetypal mystery devices such as the locked room mystery, noting how successful each entry is in delivering the goods. Biographies of the top stars appear, including information on how the star came to be attached to the series and what happened to them after they left the series. Backer also notes the introduction of directors just starting out who would go on to bigger and better things. Rising talent such as William Castle, Edward Dmytryk and Jacques Tourneur belong in that category and are profiled. Backer also includes a detailed production history of each series. Some entries employ stars popular at the moment, but others employ rising talent, some personalities easily forgotten but others were to become bigger stars once they evolved beyond the B-arena that provided them a humble start. We can read how George Sanders, who originated The Saint and The Falcon series, left The Falcon series and was replaced by his real-life brother Tom Conway, and of course, Backer compares the quality of the Falcon entries starring Sanders to those starring Conway. But most interesting, in *The Falcon's Brother* both actors appear together in the same film with the original Falcon dying at the movie's end and his surviving brother picking up the mantle and becoming the new Falcon. Backer does a wonderful job in documenting such changes in a variety of series.

Bottom line, Ron Backer does a thoroughly respectable job here, if not quite delivering the definitive job we might have been hoping for. But *Mystery Movies Series of the 1940s Hollywood* both informs and entertains. And for B-cinema, that is probably enough.

Silent Mystery and Detective Mo-vies: A Comprehensive Filmography by Ken Wlaschin; McFarland www.mcfarlandpub.com; Order 800-253-2187; 291 pages soft cover $55

McFarland is famous for publishing encyclopedic A-Z lists of films focused upon a specific topic. Ken Wlaschin presents an A-Z listing of silent film detective and mystery movies, and after a brief intro, this is exactly what the book does. Other than providing an appendix of authors whose stories were the basic of some of the silent era movies and a bibliography and index, the book covers many classics but more likely unknown, unseen and forgotten relics of the silent film era. Remember, most of these movies have been lost, so much of the research is based upon credits and cast lists and generic synopses.

For instance, let's jump to some of the classic stuff, seven versions of *Dr. Jekyll and Mr. Hyde*, at least two of which have survived—the John Barrymore and Sheldon Lewis features. Both were released in 1920 but we are told that the Barrymore version is based upon the Stevenson novella but that the Lewis version is only loosely based on the literary work, and in the synopsis Wlaschin differentiates how the plots differ. For the Lewis version he tells us: "[Jekyll] is a radical free-thinking atheist." He has "a lust to be wicked." Basically we are told the Barrymore version is an American film released by Paramount in seven reels. Besides the general synopsis, we are told the names of some of the cast and crewmembers, including the director,

the photographer and the screenwriter. We are told the film is available on video, but the specific history of home video release is absent. For the Sheldon Lewis version, again we get a relatively brief synopsis with a few cast and credits mentioned. We are told: "Some critics considered this the worst movie ever made about the story." Who these critics might be and why they felt the version to be inferior to the others is never addressed.

For Fritz Lang's avowed classic *Dr. Mabuse, der Spieler* (*Dr. Mabuse, The Gambler*) and one of the most significant mystery/detective movies of the silent era, we get only get a total of 18 lines of single column (the layout is two-column) text. Basically we are told the basic story, read the names of the cast members and discover the names of the major artists involved in bringing the movie to life. We are finally told the movie was released in two parts, as *The Gambler* and *King of Crime*.

Some of the movie coverage is as scant as six lines and the longest coverage goes as much as about 20 lines. We do have a few photographs and posters (a total of 194) spread throughout the layout. Basically, it seems that everything in this book can be found on the Internet Movie Database, and perhaps in much greater detail, with complete cast and credits list and often with more background material documented. I am sure the author lists many so-called lost silent films where only the cast and credit lists survive, since no one living today most likely saw many of the films documented.

But for a $55 price tag my point is that many of these silent movies have become classics, have survived even to this day and are available on home video—with much more specific knowledge to be had. The author opting not to have six lines on some titles and six pages on others simply achieved the dumbing down effect of writing precious little on *every* movie, even the films that warrant a more detailed observation. For the modern film fan and historian craving to come away from this book with infinite wisdom and facts, I am sorry to report this is not that book. It is woefully generic and underwritten and under-researched. Go online and get all this information plus more for free. No way is this book worth $55 in today's marketplace.

The appendix that lists and gives short biographies of the authors whose work was adapted for the silent movie screen in the mystery and detective genre, to me, is the most interesting part of the entire volume. And I am sure that such biographical data could also be culled from the Internet without too much trouble.

Today, a wealth of film information is available for free on the Internet, so it is the responsibility of today's film historians to go beyond that common knowledge and present research that warrants the price tag of the book.

In Lonely Places: Film Noir Beyond the City by Imogen Sara Smith; McFarland www.mcfarlandpub.com; Order 800-253-2187; 255 pages soft cover $45

As is generally accepted, the hard-boiled world of film noir typically occurs in urban areas, usually the corrupt big city, and the corruption of the external city is often contrasted to the corruption that brews inside the protagonist's mind. Smith, in her enthusiastic analysis of over 100 film noirs that do not occur in the big city, covers noirs that reside "in the suburbs, the small town, on the road, in the desert, borderlands and the vast, empty West." In other words, the environment of film noir is opened up to include an expanded geography of crime, corruption and fractured moral conscience.

In the thought-provoking Introduction, Smith differentiates between the more apparent trappings of the city and the less apparent yet equally oppressive life in the suburbs, and she shares examples from film noir to help illustrate her point. Pointing out that the force driving film noir is the urge to escape and that usually meant escaping from big city corruption. But as Robert Mitchum is quoted from *When Strangers Marry*: "Places are all alike; you can't run away from yourself." Smith tells us that the city is film noir's "most elaborate visual metaphor for incarceration," but that even our home can be seen as "a stifling cage." After WWII Smith elaborates on the "disappearing city" where many argued that it was now obsolete and no longer met the needs of modern life. Many Cold War fears emphasized that survival was in part dependent on the masses no longer living so close together and that suburban life was created to mimic the ideal small-town life. The so-called "enforced intimacy of the tenements" was gone, but in the suburbs so was diversity eradicated, as rows of near identical houses encouraged uniformity. Smith speaks of the "jaundiced view of suburban life" as being "soulless" and "culturally impoverished." Quoting from the movie *Tension*, men view the suburbs as an escape from their place of work with plenty of fresh air and room to entertain. In other words, men see freedom. While

the desperate wife calls her potential new suburban home "a miserable spot. It's 30-minutes from nowhere." Women see the isolation and entrapment of suburban life. The author reminds us that many noir protagonists scream to be "somebody," but that in the conformist suburban world, everyone and everything seems to be the same. In the world of film noir, the suburban environment creates a sense of creeping horror where everyone is like everyone else (one of the major themes projected by *Invasion of the Body Snatchers*, where the horrors of suburbia are explored). As Smith reminds us, in movies such as *White Heat* that occurs in the city, in the suburbs and in rural areas, the manic Cody Jarrett mourns the death of his mother by walking alone at night, speaking to her and stating how lonely he is. Later he tells another man how hard his mother's life was, "always on the run, always on the move."

From here the book gets down to its business. Chapters include: "Imaginary Prisons: Noir and the City"; "In Exile at Home: Noir Between Two Worlds"; "Maximum Security: Domestic Noir"; "The Tyranny of Neighbors: Small-Town Noir"; "Blind Highways: Noir on the

Road" and finally concludes with chapters illustrating noir on the Mexican Border, desert noir, noir Westerns and noir in the mind. Just reading the chapter headings begins to get my head spinning and interested in Smith's refreshing approach.

Quite simply, *In Lonely Places* has become one of my favorite books on film noir and I cannot emphasize just how much insight and thoughtful analysis went into its writing. It is thought provoking and intellectual, but without becoming academic or dry. It looks at many films that have been explored in other books on noir, but it somehow finds something new to say and cleverly establishes themes that Smith traces through several films at a time.

For instance, just taking a quick look at chapter four, "The Tyranny of Neighbors: Small-Town Noir," we are reminded of both Bedford Falls and Pottersville from *It's A Wonderful Life* as being Jekyll and Hyde American towns, one "friendly and harmonious" and the other "crooked and ruled by money and fear." Yet Smith reminds us that George Bailey spends most of his life trying to escape from Bedford Falls. He rebels against the "obligation and monotony" that living in the ideal small town creates.

Even though we often are attracted to dusty small towns that seem so radically different from huge urban metropolitans that frame our life today, Smith reminds us that people living in such small towns exist amid a community that "restricts freedom and encourages intolerance." The inhabitants are typed as "narrow-minded, conservative, ignorant, self-righteous and distrustful of outsiders." Such an idyllic environment then becomes simplistic rather than merely simple and the community demands its citizens absorb a rather narrow worldview. During the 1930s, the author reminds us that Hollywood often projected small-town America as places to get out of at all costs. During the 1940s, Hollywood pictured small-town America as being symbolic of American values, representing the very thing for which the troops would fight. Yet, at the same time during the war the small town was also pictured as "dangerous." With their eyes shut, how could people protect themselves against worldwide evil? How could innocent, sheltered people confront evil? Into this chapter are woven analyses of such essential film noir as *Shadow of a Doubt, The Stranger, The Desperate Hours, Storm Warning, The Well, The Lawless, The Phenix City Story, Flamingo Road, Woman in Hiding* and many, many others.

For lovers of noir, exploring the dark world of both corrupted and corrupting moral conscience by exploring the environment where the noir action occurs is gripping. It allows the viewer to better understand the urges, the fears and aspirations of characters in conflict in a new frame of reference. Even with the ability to physically move from one location to another, the haunted protagonist is imprisoned by his or her own mind and that mental or psychological prison cannot be escaped by mere physical means (running away, creating a fresh start in life by moving to another city, changing identifies, living on the road, etc.). Imogen Sara Smith has created an essential and totally absorbing look at the world of film noir and the book comes with the highest recommendation. Smith kept me glued to every page.

The Films of Donald Pleasence by Christopher Gullo; BearManor Media, P.O. Box 71426, Albany, GA 31708 (bearmanormedia.com); 302 pages soft cover $21.95

Christopher Gullo is a fan of Donald Pleasence and this, the first book devoted entirely to the late actor, demonstrates the depth of devotion he feels. The book opens with a letter of appreciation written by Pleasence's wife Linda to the author, which is followed by the author's Introduction where he lists his reasons why he wrote a book on the film (and theatrical) career of Donald Pleasence. Next is a rather dry but very thorough biography of Pleasence, peppered with many quotes, some of them from other published sources, but many of them from personal interviews conducted by the author. Such personal reflections add humanity to the actor's life story.

Then the essential book begins, a chronological listing of the actor's films (starting with *The Beachcomber* in 1954 and ending with *Fatal Frames* in 1995). The coverage of each film usually occurs over two pages of text and always follows the same template. First we get a four to five line cast list, usually ending with the director noted (but no other credits for essential, creative contributors are included). Next we get the standard synopsis, usually approaching one page of text. Finally we are offered a commentary on the film that approaches a page in length, thus dividing coverage about equally between synopsis and commentary. In today's world of film criticism and history, long, detailed synopses are generally frowned upon, especially when such coverage can easily be found on the Internet Movie Database or the lengthy film database on TCM.com. Since Pleasence's movie career started in the mid-1950s, such cast lists and synopses are very easily found for most of the films under discussion, so the first question is this. Why did Gullo not cut down on such repetitive research and focus entirely on more in-depth commentary?

For example, one of Pleasence's more renowned horror dramas is *The Flesh and the Fiends* (note—Gullo does not include any alternate titles in the main heading), released in 1960. Its coverage is generally longer than the average analysis of more ordinary films and expands slightly past three pages. Gullo's approach quotes some dialogue from the film, includes a comparison to other movies (such as Robert Wise's *The Body Snatchers*) and comparison between the facts of the film and some actual facts concerning the real-life Burke and Hare (six murders are depicted in the film but in real life the duo killed a total of 16 people). Gullo feels this is the first film where Donald Pleasence "practically steals the whole film." And thus a detailed analysis of his performance appears. In other words telling us just how he stole the film. Also, Peter Cushing's involvement and how he came to be part of the production is explained. Finally, Gullo offers some of the more gruesome aspects of the production. Basically, his is a fan's personal reflection and the analysis, since all of his films are covered, is never as

George Rose (Burke), Billie Whitelaw (Mary) and Donald Pleasence (Hare) from *The Flesh and the Fiends* (1960)

detailed as it might be in a book where fewer films were covered. The author always finds ways to discuss aspects of interest but little new information or insight is to be found.

Taking another film, the classic *Halloween*, one of Pleasence's more popular movies, we are told about the film being one of the most successful independent productions ever made and that director John Carpenter was a horror movie fan as a kid. We are told about Carpenter's style in personally scoring his own movie and some aspects that made "The Shape" so horrific. We are told about who were Carpenter's first choices to play the role of Dr. Loomis, just as Pleasence was not the first choice to play the villain in *You Only Live Twice*. Finally a close look of Pleasence playing Dr. Loomis and what he brought to the performance closes out the analysis. Once again, Gullo includes mainly boilerplate factoids and analysis. Don't get me wrong, it is an entertaining read but nothing actually new is included. We are constantly hoping to read some fresh interpretation or dazzling insight that creates a "wow" factor.

What would I like to see included in this first book on actor Donald Pleasence? First of all, I would like to see perhaps one chapter on the evolution of his Dr. Loomis character in the Halloween series, often directed and scripted at various levels of competence by diverse filmmakers. Despite such artistic distractions, how did Loomis remain faithful to the role? To me this would be interesting analysis since the series could be discussed and not each film in isolation.

Also, perhaps we need individual chapters where Pleasence's performances might be characterized into, say, four or five types of performances, where we can see a pattern between his roles in different movies over the course of several decades. We can start to analyze the dramatic scene-chewing villain vs. the subtle, introverted, internal villain. The performances where Pleasence is meek and lacks confidence vs. others where he commands the screen with his bravado. Rather than write about Pleasence in isolation, detailing each film separately, I would have taken the harder road and tried to characterize the range of performances Pleasence perfected over the course of his career and devote each chapter to a different type, and deal with six or seven movies that illustrate that type within the chapter. In this manner Gullo could go into more depth and dissect the artistic contribution of Donald Pleasence over the course of his career. That is the book on Donald Pleasence that I wish I

were reading. Christopher Gullo does an adequate job but we long for something much more than merely adequate. A complete list of Pleasence's films could be included at the end, but we do not need analysis of each and every film. Instead the thematic chapters, as described above, would produce much more food for thought and maintain interest because of the focus on performance and craft.

Wild Beyond Belief! Interviews With Exploitation Filmmakers of the 1960s and 1970s by Brian Albright; McFarland www.mcfarlandpub.com; Order 800-253-2187; 240 pages soft cover $39

Generally today too many writers use the interview as an easy way to write a book. Pick out a genre, interview (if they are still alive and willing to talk) people associated with that genre and pretty soon an author would have enough text to fill a book. Sometimes it works, but more frequently all we have is a bunch of fan boys who meet and interview celebrities at conventions and suddenly feel they are authors. The exception to the rule are interviewers such as Tom Weaver who have devoted their lives to searching out and interviewing everyone and compiling all of them in a series of book-length interviews. The problem is not the questions that Weaver asks, but the ones that he does not (if the celebrity appeared in a classic Hollywood movie, they are typically asked only questions about their horror movie work). And Brian Albright is another one of the good interviewers. His goal was to compile interviews with American exploitation filmmakers, conducted over 12 years, to create an oral history of the sub-genre. A few of the interviews appeared in truncated versions in various film magazines, but most of them are being published for the first time in this book. Albright is keen enough to notice that pretty much everyone interviewed in the book worked with at least one other (or several) of the other celebrities interviewed, producing a close-knit community of maverick moviemakers.

For instance, the first interview, "Psycho a Go-Go: Al Adamson" establishes the template of offering about one page of biographical information pertaining to the celebrity's work. From this point the interview commences. For Al Adamson we get 9 pages total. The second interview, "Blood Monster Babe: Jennifer Bishop," focuses upon an actress who appeared in many Al Adamson productions, so the Adamson legacy is more fully developed by having Bishop comment about not just her Adamson work but all her exploitation work. However, where the Adamson interview only covered nine pages, the Bishop interview covers a full 16. Granted, far less coverage has been given Jennifer Bishop over the years and her career deserves to be explored, but Al Adamson is the exploitative kingpin here and it seems a greater focus needed to be on him and his work.

What about the questions asked, what about their insight and the responses elicited? Remember, an interview book is only as good as the quality of questions asked (and even the best ones sometimes fall on deaf ears or celebrities who just aren't in the mood at the moment). For instance, in the Adamson interview Albright asks: "Were you running a nightclub when you met Sam Sherman?" and a paragraph follows where Adamson simply describes the bar. Thus, the same question has to be asked again, but in a slightly more direct way: "How did you meet Sam Sherman?" In other words the first question did not make clear that the question concerned how Adamson met Sherman, so Adamson went in a direction opposite to what the question implied. But Albright, realizing the fuzziness of the original worded question, asked it in a simplified and more direct manner. Some great questions are asked: "Where did the idea for *Satan's Sadists* come from?"; "Tell me about some members of your stock company, like Robert Dix and Buddy Cardos." and "People seem to have the idea that you spent a lot of time reassembling other pictures." For the Jennifer Bishop interview, some of the better questions Albright asked included: "Did you get along with Lon Chaney and Russ Tamblyn?" and "How did you wind up in those two films?"

Fortunately, Albright allowed his interviews to ramble on and sometimes some of the best information appears near the end, once the celebrity loosens up and perhaps comes to trust the interviewer as time goes on. Some of these interviews are in depth and go well beyond superficial information.

Within the contents of the book, some of the people interviewed include: John "Bud" Cardos, Robert Dix, Ross Hagen, Sid Haig, Monte Hellman, Jack Hill, Gary Kent, Joyce King, Anthony Lanza, Gary Littlejohn, Bart Patton, Sam Sherman, Megan Timothy and James Gordon White.

If exploitation movies of the 1960s and '70s are your forte, then Brian Albright's book of interviews is an oral history of keen interest. Albright manages to get his subjects talking and he is wise enough to listen and let them do the bulk of the work. *Wild Beyond Belief* does a wonderful job in letting the fan in on an era of moviemaking that makes Roger Corman look like Martin Scorsese, but the anecdotes and enthusiasm shared becomes infectious and easily draws the reader in. For fans of the sub-genre, this is more than a worthwhile read.

MAD ABOUT MOVIES
HOME VIDEO REVIEW

BY GARY J. SVEHLA

Ratings: Excellent 4; Good 3; Fair 2; Poor 1

The Films of Budd Boetticher Box Set
The Tall T (3.5);
Decision at Sundown (3.5);
Buchanan Rides Alone (3.0);
Ride Lonesome (2.5);
Comanche Station (2.5)
Disc: 4.0
Sony

One of my favorite movie revelations of the past few years has been discovering, for the first time, the joy of 1950s Westerns. While I was watching Universal and Hammer horror movies theatrically as a child, these Westerns, released at precisely the same time, went unnoticed by my crowd. But such is not the case any longer.

About two years ago I learned of B-director Budd Boetticher when his first Randolph Scott Western, *Seven Men from Now*, was released to DVD. Harry Joe Brown produced the series, with star Randolph Scott as co-producer. Burt Kennedy (soon to become a Western director of renown a decade later) wrote many of the screenplays, with Charles Lang writing the rest, but visionary Budd Boetticher created a unified vision for all the Western films he directed. Yes, all were 80-minute B-movies, made on a modest budget, populated with rising stars-to-be (or stars on their way down). But his films featured complexities of morality, cast shadowy lines between heroes and villains and used the canvas of Technicolor and widescreen photography to deliver the goods. Star Randolph Scott, not a young man by the mid-1950s, most resembles the quiet dignity of Gary Cooper in *High Noon*. While Scott walks erect with a swagger and a prideful smile, he is seldom in no-holds-barred fistfights, and while he wins at the quick draw, his victory is more due to editing than innate skill. These Boetticher Westerns were intended for the now aging adults who cut their teeth on the juvenile B antics of Hopalong Cassidy, Roy Rogers and Gene Autry.

The Tall T, released in 1957, features Scott as Pat Brennan, a man simply attempting to stay alive. Unlike most Western heroes that are made to appear larger than life, Brennan loses his horse in a bet where he attempts to ride and tame a bucking bull—and gets thrown. While the cowhands point and laugh at his failure, Brennan, shy and slightly embarrassed, maintains his dignity and sense of humor and—saddlebags in hand—marches on foot across the desert. A privately rented stagecoach housing newlyweds Willard (John Hubbard) and Doretta (Maureen O'Sullivan) Mims pick him up. It seems the spinsterish Doretta married Willard as her last shot for romance and domestic bliss, but the wily Willard married for money (Doretta being the daughter of one of the richest men in the territory). Willard, not happy about picking up Brennan, reluctantly does so. Shortly thereafter three outlaws—leader Usher (Richard Boone, star of the TV series *Have Gun Will Travel*) and his two bloodthirsty guns, Billy Jack (Skip Homeier) and Chink (a youthful Henry Silva)—rob the stagecoach. What at first seems to have

been a happenstance robbery soon turns dark and complex. It seems that Willard hired the outlaw gang to hold his wife for ransom, forcing a big payoff from her rich daddy. When Doretta discovers the truth, she is overcome with bitterness and hatred, but Brennan, who admires the woman, reminds her that only her pride has been injured and that the main idea is to stay alive.

The theme of moral ambiguity comes to prominence, as it does in all Boetticher Westerns, when the moral yet practical Brennan has heart-to-heart chats with the immoral yet practical Usher. Usher declares that he never does any of the killing, that he allows the dirty work to be done by loose canons Billy Jack and Chink. Usher makes a point to Brennan that he has kept Brennan alive, even though the young punks want him dead. When Brennan reminds Usher that he runs with the toughs and is tainted, Usher admits that he does, and that he gives in to their evil because of such association. Usher is the type of man who knows better, realizes his corruption and soiled character, but for practical reasons accepts his fate as being one of the damned. Even so, in one conversation with Brennan, Usher, with that far away look in his eye, speaks of a dream of owning his own place. But Usher soon rides out to make the deal with Doretta's father, while Brennan and Doretta remain alone with Billy Jack and Chink. Brennan realizes he has limited time to overtake and kill the young guns before Usher returns. But by using his mind (not his brawn), he does just that.

Violence in Boetticher's universe is almost Val Lewtonesque. Instead of showing us bloodshed and gore, Boetticher suggests the worst of fates by painting us a picture. In the movie's opening, Brennan stops by the way station to visit a father and his son, the boy offering Brennan money to buy him candy in town. The father, expressing loneliness since his wife died, says he comes up for retirement next fall and that he will take it. He feels this is not a good life for his boy and him. But when Usher and his cohorts overtake that station, Brennan later inquires about the safety of the man and his boy, and Usher points to the well. The camera simply lingers on the well, yet not one body is ever shown. But the idea resonates that an innocent father, nearing retirement, and his fresh-bud boy met violent deaths. When Brennan and Billy Jack struggle later over a rifle, the rifle fires hitting the outlaw in the head. We never see any blood or any squid explosions. As Doretta runs into the room, Brennan orders her to look away. Later, Usher is hit in the face by shotgun blast, but we only see him fall and cover his face in pain, until he expires. Violence and the pain of violence is vividly suggested but seldom shown.

The climax shows the difficulty Brennan has in killing Usher. Brennan, mounted on his horse, has the jump on the outlaw, but Usher constantly reminds Brennan that he is responsible for having kept him alive so long. Indecision painted all over his face, Brennan holds his shotgun firmly on Usher, itching to do away with him, as the confident Usher tells Brennan to keep the money, that all he wants to do is ride away and forget that this ever happened. Brennan allows just that, but once Usher passes a rocky hill, he snatches a rifle from his saddlebag and turns around to reclaim his booty. But Brennan, still holding the shotgun in position, is the lucky one and scores the killing shot.

Even though shot in Technicolor, *The Tall T* is burdened with excessive grain (seen mostly in the blue sky) that undermines the quality of the digital print. The Tech hues are not as intense as they should be, but overall, the quality of the print is very nice, yet not as nice as one might hope.

The second film in the series, *Decision at Sundown*, improves the digital print quality. Again, we have heavy grain in several sequences, but the print is more colorful, more vibrant and appears to be closer to actual 35mm Technicolor.

Decision at Sundown, again released in 1957, features a screenplay by Charles Lang. The theme of moral ambiguity is even more prominent and taints our hero, Bart Allison (Randolph Scott). It seems that Allison and partner Sam (Noah Beery, Jr.) are heading to the town of Sundown for revenge. Good-natured (and comic relief) Sam is unaware of why, because tight-lipped Allison's intensity and squinty-eyed stoic expression say back off to even his closest friends. Allison is headed to town to attend the wedding of Tate Kimbrough (John Carroll), the titular leader of the town and a corrupting influence. Strangely, the B-film never explains how Kimbrough is a corrupting force, but all the town citizens act whipped and listless and speak of having lost their self-respect. Everyone hangs out at the town saloon, drinking nonstop, and the affable barkeep keeps muttering something about losing faith in humanity. Kimbrough is a scamp, a womanizer and most likely a tyrant, but he is also a well-mannered gentleman who relishes power. Before the wedding, the movie's scarlet lady, well-named Ruby (Valerie French), who obviously loves and has been having an affair with Kimbrough, announces she will be attending the wedding, to Kimbrough's chagrin. She faces him head on and states that she has given him more than a woman should give a man, but that still wasn't enough to make him want to marry her. But for her own self-respect, she feels she must attend the ceremony. Kimbrough, a wonderful cad, asks her one last favor, to please not sit in the front row. The bride-to-be, a beautiful trophy wife Lucy (Karen Steele), is not the object of Kimbrough's lust but the object of his gaining respectability, her father Charles being an important community and business leader. However, before the wedding begins, while all the guests wait impatiently in the pews, an intense Allison storms into the church and announces he has reason why the wedding should not take place. Soon the outraged and embarrassed Kimbrough orders his paid-for-sheriff Swede (Andrew Duggan) to kill the interloper. Of course Allsion and Sam barricade themselves in the town's livery stable, fending off the law, even wounding a deputy. Swede refuses to charge the stable as ordered by Kimbrough, so for the bulk of the film the plot concerns this dramatic standoff.

A running gag is that poor Sam never has a chance to get a meal, and he is starving. But he gets a chance after Allison forces his buddy to leave. The reason for Allison's revenge is that, when he went away during the Civil War, his wife begun an illicit affair with Kimbrough. Before he returned home, she killed herself in shame. Sam knows the truth that Allison's wife was no good, that she entertained many other men, not only Kimbrough. When given the chance to ride out of town unharmed, Allison forces Sam to leave and accept the deal, and Sam heads to the local restaurant for endless eggs. However, after he finishes his meal, he is gunned down, shot in the back, as the good town citizens simply sit by and watch. This senseless murder only fuels Allison's passions, but the truth is that Sam was correct and that Kimbrough is not the total bastard that Allison paints him out to be. In fact, in Boetticher's universe, the hero is tainted by denial and rage and becomes a flawed man in the sense that Kimbrough is a flawed man as well. In the Boetticher universe villains are typically the most complex and finely drawn characters.

However, Allison's courage to confront the town dictator gives renewed courage to the ensemble cast of good town people (including character actors James Westerfield, Ray Teal, Vaughn Taylor, Richard Deacon, etc.) to regain their self respect by rising up and righting the wrongs of the past several years. The town doctor (John Archer) becomes the prime mover and shaker, but Morley Chase (Ray Teal) and his boys intercede and even the odds, making sure no one shoots Allison in the back. Also showing courage is baddie Tate Kimbrough. Realizing he is finished in this town, Kimbrough decides, for his pride, to strap on his guns and leave town by walking out to the town square, board his buggy (with partner Ruby, at long last) and ride slowly away, giving a nod and smile to the town citizenry. Yes, the villain gets out of town alive, but Boetticher has made it clear, no black and white simplistic heroes and villains exist in this film.

After Kimbrough leaves and all the citizens are drinking in the saloon, slapping one another on the back for their renewed moral courage, the still cranky Allison throws his whiskey glass against the bar, smashing the mirror, claiming if they had only acted with courage before his friend Sam was gunned down in the streets, Sam would be here celebrating too. Instead, as the doctor notes when Allison rides out of town, Allison did lots for this town, but unfortunately, there's not much we could do for him. And on such a serious thought, the somber film ends without a happy resolution.

When 1958 arrived, Boetticher returned with *Buchanan Rides Alone*, another film scripted by Charles Lang, and this time photographed by Lucien Ballard in Columbia Color (not Technicolor). But the color has been nicely restored. While some grain remains in the print, overall, the digital print looks beautiful.

Unfortunately, *Buchanan Rides Alone* becomes the least of the first three films, but it showcases the already established Boetticher themes. Interestingly enough, it seems all of these films begin with Randolph Scott's character riding into a strange town at the beginning and

exiting at the end. Here Randolph Scott's Tom Buchanan is not a man with a sordid, haunted past, but a smiling man with $2,000 in coin in his gun belt, headed back home to West Texas. For this pleasant character, he just winds up in the wrong place at the wrong time. Buchanan rides into the American border town of Agry, a town controlled by the three Agry brothers, corrupt and shady as they come. First off we have Judge Simon Agry, the titular town leader, a man of wealth and position, plotting a run for political office (becoming governor of the state is not beyond his grasp). However, Abe Carbo, the gentleman gunfighter, has the judge's back and does his dirty work. The town sheriff is brother Lew Agry, a man whose corruption becomes a tad more transparent as he and his deputies are not above hanging an innocent man, just as an excuse to steal his money. The third brother, Amos, is the lowest gene pool member of the clan, resembles the Andy Devine "Jingles" character from TV and B-Westerns. Amos is overweight, not too bright and his performance requires his character to run all over the town, out of breath, pressing his hand to his breast. When the only son of the judge is shot down in the town saloon by Juan de la Vega (Manuel Rojas) for committing an unspoken crime (a sister's rape is hinted at), Juan is arrested, but so is Buchanan, who has revealed to Amos the amount of money he is carrying around town. Since Bu-

A Belgian movie poster for *Ride Lonesome*

chanan came to the Mexican's aide when Lew and his men were roughing the kid up, Lew arrests Buchanan, citing the two men worked together to murder the boy, so both will hang. But we all know the reason for the frame is to kill Buchanan so the Agry boys can split his money for themselves (that is Lew and Amos, as Simon is already wealthy).

However, during the trial, Buchanan is found innocent and freed, almost. Still motivated by the money, Lew orders Buchanan out of town immediately, without his gun or money, escorted by the deputies whose job it will be to assassinate the innocent man. However, one of the deputies, Pecos (L.Q. Jones), also comes from West Texas and bonds with Buchanan, so when the time comes to shoot Buchanan in the back no less, Pecos does the right thing and shoots the other deputy. For his loyalty Buchanan offers Pecos half of his stake, but the deputy does not live much longer to enjoy his spoils.

Instead of presenting the theme of moral ambiguity front and center, here we experience the Agry brother feud, where Simon and Lew fight over the possession of outlaw Juan, whose wealthy father is willing to pay $50,000 to get his son back. Simon brokers the money deal, willing to accept the bounty for the death of his son (who no doubt deserved his comeuppance). Buchanan, who befriends and helps Juan escape and return home, is caught up in the mess because Lew and Amos need him dead so they can steal his money. And Lew connives to capture Juan so he can collect the $50,000, not Simon. The character that represents the theme of moral ambiguity is Carbo (Craig Stevens), the gunman who covers Simon's back. Buchanan and Carbo have a few encounters, stuffed with moralistic dialogue, but unfortunately, the spotlight shines brightly on the Agry feud and Carbo's character is not fully developed. Strangely, in a Budd Boetticher movie, the character we suspect should become the film's primary focus instead remains a borderline character.

The tension explodes in the climax with Buchanan and Juan on one side of the street and the Agry boys and Carbo on the other, while the saddlebag of $50,000 lies between them. As both sides attempt to snatch the saddlebag, more victims pile up dead, including two of the three Agry boys. At the film's end, Buchanan, back in possession of both his money and gun, is ready to ride out of town, conceding to Carbo that the town now belongs to him. As Carbo, a glint in his eye, agrees, Buchanan, a glint in his, mutters that he wouldn't have any part of this town, as he rides out alone. For the first time Randolph Scott's character seems almost ordinary, driven by his need to reclaim his money and perhaps help the young Mexican. The town's corruption is a tad too formulaic, too pat, and the character that needed to be better developed remains woefully neglected. The film, only 80 minutes long, seems to drag slightly in the middle, even though for a B-Western *Buchanan Rides Alone* is above the standard.

By 1959, with *Ride Lonesome*, Budd Beotticher was credited as producer and director, with Harry Joe Brown listed as executive producer. No credit mentions Randolph Scott being co-producer. However, the film is credited to Ranown Productions, and this includes Scott's participation. Boetticher was now filming his Westerns in actual CinemaScope, and in this movie and the following one, *Comanche Station*, Boetticher seems to be taking himself more seriously and imitating the style of John Ford with those panoramic outdoor shots where the clouds and rocky bluffs loom large and people on wagon and horseback seem so small and far away. The spirit and fun of *Buchanan Rides Alone* is gone, and these last two Westerns, scripted by Burt Kennedy, bear a lethargic and depressed tone. Instead of making fun, action-packed B-productions, Boetticher seems to want to make statement pictures, but on a very limited budget. Many fans and critics love these final two Westerns and think they show the full artistic range of Boetticher's capabilities, but for me, I enjoy the first three movies in this box set the most.

Ride Lonesome is a very interesting movie nonetheless, and the acting is exceptional. James Best, known more for his teenage and sci-fi exploitation movies, demonstrates his talent in the role of villain Billy John (he is known for shooting victims in the back). In the film's opening sequence, he allows bounty hunter Ben Brigade (Randolph Scott) to sneak up on him, claiming his gang of five are spread out in the rocky hills nearby, ready to gun Brigade down on his order. Brigade, grim and serious, states that could happen, but that he would cut John in half as he is falling. In a wonderful sequence, Best screams out to the wilderness for his men to back off, uttering an angry little aside claiming he knew their plan would never work, as the cuffs are slapped on the smiling outlaw. But Billy screams out for his boys to tell older brother Frank what is going down. Frank will know what to do. Meanwhile Brigade and Billy travel to an isolated stagecoach station, to find it manned by two outlaws: Sam (Pernell Roberts) and sidekick Whit (James Coburn, looking terribly youthful and skinny), and the wife (Karen Steele) of the stationmaster awaits her husband's return. Soon the wife, Mrs. Lane, learns the tragic fate of her husband, but Sam and Whit tell Brigade that they want to travel close to him. It seems a reward is being offered to turn in Billy and amnesty is offered to any outlaw who does the job. Sam, one of those complex, multi-leveled villains that are prominent in Boetticher Westerns, speaks about reaching middle age and wanting to have something to call his own, the desire to own land and some cattle. Because of his outlaw past, such a dream can never be, but if he kills Brigade and brings Billy in, he will be a free man. Slower-witted Whit asks if he can work for Sam on his new ranch, and Sam tells him, in sudden intensity, no. Then he smiles and tells Whit that he can't work for him because he will be his partner. So, once again, Boetticher crafts an outlaw with regrets, morality and a sense of fair play. However, his means of getting Billy just does not seem righteous.

However, Brigade has a plan of his own. As is true of most Randolph Scott characters in Boetticher Westerns, Brigade is a haunted man, a man who was the law years ago and saw Frank Boone kidnap his wife and hang her from the nearest hanging tree. When Brigade captured Billy, he knew all the time that crafty Frank would attempt to track his brother's captor down. Brigade isn't interested in the bounty but desires a confrontation between Frank and himself, to avenge the death of his innocent wife all those many years ago. Because of this rationale, it is not difficult for Brigade to turn over Billy to Sam and Whit at the film's conclusion, Brigade declaring, "I have no further use of him." These are solemn words spoken after Brigade and Frank (the iconic Lee Van Cleef) meet at the hanging tree, Frank finding it difficult remembering hanging the former lawman's wife. Frank is cold but not altogether evil, willing to sacrifice his life to try to save his brother and acting honorably to allow Brigade to avenge his wife's death. Frank is a criminal but somewhat a man of honor. Sam Boone, highly likable and moralistic, is an outlaw who matured, who learned the folly of one's youth might be corrected by making better choices in middle age. Whether Sam would have gunned down Brigade to claim Billy for himself is never known, but when Brigade willingly turns the man over, warning Sam that he'd better go straight or else he will hunt him down, Sam greets the kindness with gratitude, graciousness and humbleness. Poor Billy is the only pawn in this game that is getting the shaft, but well he deserves it. Unfortunately, too much of *Ride Lonesome* is filled with idle chatter, long rides across the plains, majestic yet interminable outdoor landscape shots and suspense mounting with very little action. It's as though Boetticher forgot what people look for in Westerns and instead tried to get too serious and heavy, losing the artistic balance that was better captured in the earlier films.

In 1960s's *Comanche Station*, Budd Boetticher seems to be replicating the look and feel of the first third of *The Searchers*, trying to mimic, on a smaller scale, the photographic look of those Monument Valley sequences with the renegade Comanche in the background and the U.S. Calvary in the foreground. Boetticher was filming in Alabama and not in Arizona, and his cast was much smaller. But we have the Cody party (Randolph Scott) crossing the plains as the Comanche loom above them in the background, ready to attack. As the Cody party tries to remain calm and not panic, Cody yells, at a specific moment, for his party to run like hell, a sequence very similar to one in *The Searchers*. Again using CinemaScope photography, Boetticher likes to frame his shots emphasizing the tremendous and overwhelming landscape that dwarf the human travelers. It's not exactly John Ford, but four years after that Western classic, Beotticher is paying homage or being influenced by one of the great Westerns of all time. The truth is that Boetticher is best when he is pure Boetticher and not reminding the viewer of some other Western classic.

Here, Cody is a loner, traveling through Comanche territory, awaiting the appearance of the Comanche tribe, so he can trade blankets, triviality and a rifle for a white woman they have held captive. The woman Nancy (Nancy Gates), obviously sexually abused by the tribe bucks, is worse for wear, but her husband is offering a huge ransom for her return. Cody cannot understand why the husband does not go out and find her himself, but the viewer is not sure that Cody is acting entirely altruistically or whether the bounty is his prime motivator.

Comanche Station is perhaps the least of the movies in this collection, and while it trances Boetticher's themes estab-

lished in earlier works, it remains slightly derivative of better movies and tends to meander. All of Boetticher's Westerns are worth viewing, don't get me wrong, but this one seems slight. However, when the collected Westerns of Budd Boetticher are taken together, we have a Western cinema auteur whose work, too long neglected, can stand heads and tails against the work of the A-production cinema masters. Boetticher, working in the world of low-budget cinema, brings a universe of complexity and hard moral decisions to a B-movie genre that formerly thrived on simple male camaraderie and tales of black and white moral decisions where the outlaws typically telegraph their evil intentions by wearing black hats (unless the hero is Hopalong Cassidy!). While Boetticher never had the resources given John Ford or Howard Hawks and others, he took what he was given and created a body of Westerns that will stand the test of time.

Westbound
Film: 3.0; Disc: 3.5
Warner Archive Collection

What a boon!

After the Budd Boetticher box set of Randolph Scott Westerns was released, following the initial single film release of *Seven Men from Now*, the Western that sparked the re-discovery of the B-Western series of Randolph Scott Westerns direct-

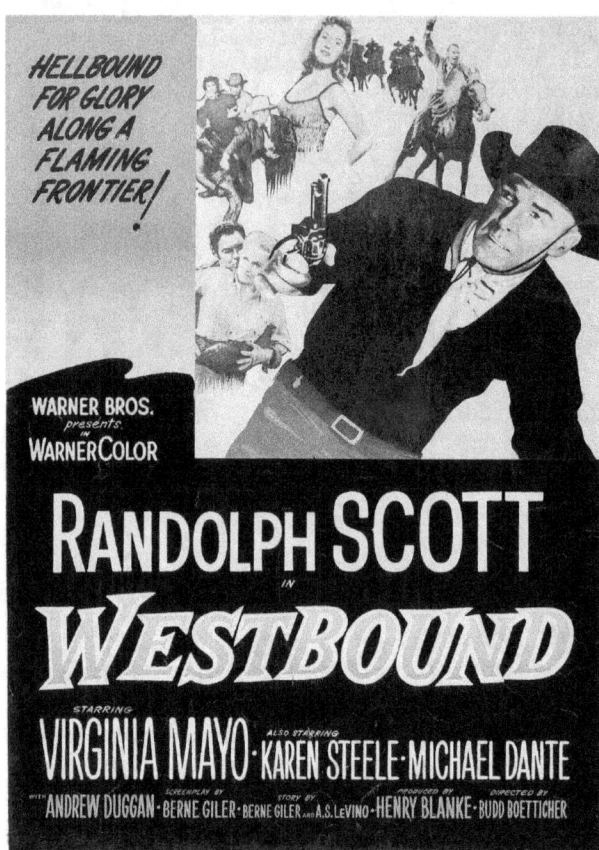

ed by Boetticher, now comes the MOD-DVD release of 1959's *Westbound*, the next to last film the team created. Now all of Budd Boetticher's Randolph Scott Westerns are available on DVD release.

Returning once again to Warner Bros., Boetticher did not work from a screenplay by his repertory company writers, instead Berne Giler wrote the screenplay based upon his novel. This brought freshness to the series, even though Boetticher milked the story for all its moral ambiguity and other signature touches.

In this complex story, it is 1864 and the War Between the States is raging, with the North being squeezed by the Confederates, who are preventing their gold shipments moving from the West to the East. Superiors tell Army captain John Hayes (Randolph Scott) that the process of shipping gold via stagecoach East will be accelerated, and that Hayes is in the dubious position of taking charge of the entire operation, making sure the gold is protected and arrives in a timely manner. In his wonderful opening dialogue, Hayes refuses the position, understanding full well that the government's desperate actions are trouble bound and that he does not want the aggravation. However, the military insists, and off goes the reluctant officer to Julesburg, Colorado, where he finds the rich, titular town leader Putnam (a particularly oily Andrew Duggan) married to his former girlfriend. Putnam formerly owned and operated the stagecoach company, but he suddenly resigned and sold off the horses and the way stations. Hayes learns pretty fast that the good citizens of Julesburg support the South and actively undermine the activities of the Yankees whenever they can.

Hayes befriends a young married soldier, a casualty of war, who returned with only one arm. The valiant man Rod (Michael Dante) operates a farm with his sexy young wife Janie (Karen Steele), but Rod discovers only too soon that farming with one arm is a fruitless effort. However, Hayes hires him to work for him, to operate the stagecoach way station, which he can do, even learning to cock and aim his rifle with one arm. However, Putnam's hired goon squad is headed by gunslinger Mace (the Australian Michael Pate, who would play the vampire cowboy in *The Curse of the Undead* the same year), a fast-gun who humiliates Hayes in the middle of town.

The film's strength lies in the wonderful characterizations submitted by a cast of talented professionals, especially the long-in-the-tooth Randolph Scott as the lone force of justice. Putnam, interestingly drawn, wants to undermine Hayes' efforts in every way he can, short of murder and physical violence. He thinks he has Mace and his gang under control, but Mace admits he does not care which side wins, for he is in it for the money and it does not matter who gets hurt. In a tragic sequence, the likable Rod gets gunned down when he opens the door to the way station and takes a bullet intended for Hayes. His shirt exploding in red crimson, the poor boy lingers for days until he finally expires, his wife heartbroken. Even the cold Putnam is disgusted that his anti-bloodshed orders have not been followed, and he too takes out after Mace in his speeding buggy, demonstrating that the Civil War created a warped, complex scenario of right and wrong where even some evil-doers followed moral rules (although Mace makes a superb Western villain).

Whether or not Boetticher is contrasting the degrees of evil displayed by Mace and Putnam, examining the complex man-woman relationships existing between Norma Putnam (Virginia Mayo) and the two men in her life (her husband and Hayes), or exploring the more traditional young love experienced between husband and wife Rod and Jeanie, Boetticher keeps the action building while his focus remains on intricate character development.

Westbound, with its widescreen photography and intense WarnerColor, takes a different approach to the War Between the States, and this Western shoot-'em-up maintains the perfect balance of character, plot and action to again make us appreciate Budd Boetticher's take on the American West even more.

Brute Force
Movie: 3.5; Disc: 3.5
Criterion

Director Jules Dassin and screenwriter Richard Brooks teamed up to produce one of the best psychological portraits of life within a penitentiary, 1947's *Brute Force*, a superbly-acted movie starring Burt Lancaster, Hume Cronyn, Charles Bickford and an ensemble cast that more than rises to the occasion (a youthful Whit Bissell plays a sympathetic prisoner who hangs himself in his cell). In emotional flashback sequences we see the current prisoners interact with their women outside to explain how they ended up in prison. We see the soldier who takes the blame when his girl shoots and kills an informer; we see a lovesick puppy of a man embezzle money to buy gifts for his girl; we see the gangster who loves his wheelchair bound gal so much that he will not tell her about his vices; etc. *Brute Force* does not feature any psychopathic prisoners; no monsters exist inside these cell walls. Indeed, the title *Brute Force* refers to Captain Munsey, played to perfection by diminutive actor Hume Cronyn, who thrives on savagery and power and gets the upper hand on prisoners by forcing them to be his informers. In a few pivotal sequences, Munsey tries to crack a prisoner by beating him to a pulp with a rubber hose, yet the prisoner maintains his loyalty to his friends. In a few sequences Munsey seems sympathetic and fatherly, but behind closed doors we see his evil machinations and manipulative efforts to undermine the current warden, Munsey positioning himself to be his replacement. The current warden is tentative and fails to run a tight ship, so Munsey, thinking ahead, becomes the bastard that he perceives his superiors desire for the job.

Burt Lancaster as Joe Collins becomes the impetus for escape, working with his fellow prison cellmates. His theory, shared by Howard Duff's Soldier character, involves having two gangs attack the prison tower from two different directions at the same time. Collins claims the prison guards cannot possibly defend themselves from that type of assault. Collins trusts the veteran prisoner Gallager (Charles Bickford), an honest man who plays straight with both the prisoners and the prison authorities, and whose parole is due at any time. However, when paroles are frozen, Collins knows that Gallager is ripe to play along. Bickford, operating from the mechanics shop inside, and Collins, working from the underground job site outside, coordinate their assault for the following Tuesday at 12:15 p.m. Bickford's men create firebombs and get handguns, while Collins and his team will overpower the guards and get their weapons. However, the plan is doomed from the start because one of Collins' men, unknown even to the audience, is an informer and Munsey knows everything about their plan. During the spectacular prison assault sequence, sympathetic men are cut down in their tracks, even though the prison tower is firebombed and set ablaze. Bickford dies in his truck attempting to ram the gate, and Collins, sneaking into the tower, is shot yet still manages to throw the evil Munsey off the tower, both men dying as a result. Most of the other prisoners from both camps succumb to violent and horrible deaths.

The drunken prison physician (Art Smith), a man who hates Munsey and who tips off Collins that Munsey knows of their escape plan even before they

A montage from *Brute Force*; note the calendar girl in the middle.

carry it out, becomes the movie's heart and soul. Dr. Walters knows it's the end of the line for him, being assigned to this hellhole prison, and he rebels against the higher authorities whenever he can, no matter what the price. At the end the doctor questions why the men committed such a suicidal act of desperation. He faces toward the camera and states, in the most bitter of tones, no one escapes from prison. Just as he knows prisoners never truly escape, he also knows that as long as men remain in jail they will continue to *try* to escape, even using the most desperate of ill-fated plans.

An almost corpse like calendar girl, posted in Burt Lancaster's over-crowded cell, becomes a symbol of their humanity. When punch drunk new prisoner Coy (Jack Overman) arrives, the men tell him that this girl reminds each prisoner of the specific girl left behind, and that all the men can see their own girl's image in that generic painting. That calendar girl art becomes a symbol of humanity, of life outside, that binds all the diverse criminal population into one common band of friends. In fact, before leaving his cell for the very last time, Collins rolls it up and slips the calendar beneath his shirt. He is willing to leave every thread of his prison life behind him, but not that image, not that girl.

Brute Force is tough as nails and hard-hitting, and for 1947 very violent. But at its core are souls, tortured men, who are paying the price for crimes that never deserve the fate they suffer. Each prisoner is depicted as flawed, but each man becomes sympathetic and worthy of compassion. And this complex character study of a broken culture becomes a superb movie, because it makes us think and feel. Extras include audio commentaries, an analysis of the movie by an actual criminologist who studies movies about people in prisons and trailers, etc. As usual, the print measures up to excellent Criterion standards.

The Woman in the Window
Movie: 3.0; Disc: 3.5
MGM

Following the lead of 20th Century Fox and Warner Bros., MGM came late to the game with its own series of classic film noir, and the excellent Fritz Lang feature *The Woman in the Window* is a gem. The feature stars Edgar G. Robinson

and shares similarities to his Fritz Lang-directed *Scarlett Street*, to be released one year later. But *The Woman in the Window* is the more eccentric of the two.

Imagine if *The Wizard of Oz* were recast as film noir ... not the entire screenplay itself but its inspired gimmick, with the framing story linking Dorothy's relatives and friends in dreary Kansas to the colorful people she meets in Oz

Edward G. Robinson plays a middle-aged associate professor of psychology, Richard Wanley, whose interests include the criminal mind. Sending his matronly wife and two beautiful children off for a holiday visit, Wanley joins his oldest friends for dinner in a restaurant that contains a lounge and library reading room where after-dinner drinks are served. D.A. Lalor (Raymond Massey), Dr. Barkstane (Edmund Breon) and Wanley speak of the provocative painting of a bare-shouldered model that hangs in the front window of the nearby art studio. The men speak about how the mysteries and intense passions of life have properly passed them by and that they are fools for lusting over such a portrait, as Lalor and Barkstane caught Wanley doing just before joining them for dinner. Self described "old crocs," Wanley lingers behind as his colleagues exit, Wanley wanting to enjoy a little reading and a drink. He tells his server to remind him when it is 10:30, just in case he falls asleep.

In a very noir-like course of events, Wanley exits the lounge, lingers over the enticing model painting a little longer, but this time he confronts the painting's living, breathing and sizzling subject, who watches as the professor obsesses over the painting of her. She invites him out for a drink, only one drink, but eventually invites him to her apartment to see other sketches. While downing a few too many drinks and looking over the sketches, an irate middle-aged man bursts into the girl's apartment, very upset over the presence of Wanley. A fight ensues with Wanley plunging a knife into the intruder's back, killing him. The hastily concocted scheme of hiding the body just off a rural road in a seldom traveled wooded section results. However, the unskilled criminal mind of Wanley leaves muddy tire tracks in the dirt near the murder scene, and of course, Wanley's buddy D.A. Lalor is assigned the case. Lalor even goes as far as inviting Wanley to accompany him to the crime scene, with Wanley trying to hide the cut on his hand after Lalor finds blood on a metal barb near the location where the corpse is found. Pretty soon a mental game of cat and mouse results with Wanley and Lalor slowly coming to suspect what the other man knows or suspects about the case.

When the murder appears in the press, smarmy private detective Heidt (Dan Duryea) appears on the scene. He was hired to tail the artist model Alice Reed (Joan Bennett) by the murder victim, to see if she was fooling around with any other men. Heidt quickly deduces that Wanley and Reed are involved in the murder and blackmail ensues with the oily P.I. demanding $5,000 cash by tomorrow night. Wanley and Reed, using a strong sleeping powder that Wanley acquires from his friend Dr. Barkstane, attempt to poison Heidt, but the detective is too savvy.

Phoning the professor, Reed announces the glum result, confessing she gave Heidt the $5,000 and relays to Wanley his demand for an additional $5,000 the next day. Wanley is totally depressed, and he empties packet after packet of the sleeping medicine into his glass of water, suicide obviously on his mind. In the meanwhile the police have been tailing Heidt and a gun-battle pursues. Heidt is shot and killed on the spot, his death witnessed by the horrified (and relieved) Reed. She quickly prances down the street and phones the good news to Wanley, but his eyes are half-closed, he is barely conscious and the professor quickly succumbs to the deadly sleeping potion. If the film ended on this bleak note *The Window in the Window* would be considered top-notch noir, although one of the most depressing ones ever produced.

But here's where *The Wizard of Oz* noir-isms enter!

As the professor's head slumps downward, the same waiter who served his after-dinner drink shakes him to consciousness and reminds Wanley that it is now 10:30. Surprise! Wanley never left the restaurant. He simply fell asleep reading his book and dreamed the entire noir tale. But there's more. As he fetches his hat from the hatcheck booth, the man behind the booth turns out to be the angry man he murdered from his dream. Venturing outside, an energetic cabbie approaches Wanley, and it turns out to be Dan Duryea (Heidt), but Wanley prefers to walk home alone. Of course he stops to gawk one more time at the painting of the woman hanging in the window, but this time a real floozy emerges from the shadows and asks the professor for a light, flirtatiously. Wanley, having learned his lesson, tells her no, and the movie ends with Wanley literally running down the street, getting the hell away from his bad dream!

Nunnally Johnson's inspired screenplay takes the film noir genre and flip-flops things on its ear, creating a true sendup that is not revealed to be a sendup until the last minutes of the film. Audiences probably watched the film and groaned, stating what are the odds that Wanley and his D.A. friend would be driving to the murder scene together? What are the odds that another middle-aged Romeo would be invading Reed's love nest at exactly the same time that she is trying to seduce Wanley? And isn't it a great coincidence that a private investigator just happens to be watching Reed, hired to do so by the murder victim? Too many plot coincidences exist, but as seen from the point of view of a man dreaming, it all makes perfect sense. Fritz Lang's direction is exciting and suspenseful, especially in the sequence when Duryea offers to forgo the blackmail money if Joan Bennett agrees to fly south of the border with him, while she mixes a poisonous cocktail for him, one that he hesitates to drink. And the suspense is just as taut in the woods sequence, with Massey and Robinson checking out the clues the police have found to capture the killer, with Robinson desperately trying to hide his stark reactions and fear. A master like Lang wrings every nervous moment out of such sequences.

The Woman in the Window features a pristine and dense print that accentuates the noir photography and wonderful performances. Edward G. Robinson is wonderful in his subtle performance and Fritz Lang's direction keeps the proceedings crisp and dramatic. True, *The Woman in the Window* is a gimmicky movie, but even once the gimmick is ignored, what remains is truly inspiring and gripping.

Rio Bravo
Movie: 3.5; Disc: 3.5
Warner Home Video

When it comes to the best John Wayne movies, *Rio Bravo* is always counted among the top, and well it belongs there. Most definitely *The Searchers* offers the richer character for Wayne, the brooding and deeply haunted Ethan Edwards, and for my money *The Searchers* gets the nod as being Wayne's finest performance and best movie by virtue of being the better photographed, directed, scripted and acted production. But *Rio Bravo*, released two years after *The Searchers* in 1958, is simply more fun and offers Wayne's character, John T. Chance, as more mythic and iconic, a true hero. Both films have the same period John Wayne look and Technicolor hues, but each film exists in an entirely different universe, both of which deserve constant revisiting.

Rio Bravo becomes a steely character study and a suspense thriller disguised as a Western. The basic trio of Walter Brennan as Stumpy, Dean Martin as Dude and Ricky Nelson as Colorado, working with John T. Chance, become the boys club that represents law and order. After locking up the crazed Joe Burdette (Claude Akins), Chance and his crew are in hot water as Joe's brother Nathan (John Russell of TV's *Lawman*), the titular corrupt town boss, does his best to hire professionals to kill the sheriff and his deputies to free his brother. While the gimpy Stumpy is around for comic relief (and Brennan has never been more effective in a performance that is both funny and emotionally moving), in many ways the movie belongs to Dean Martin whose fragile Dude, Chance's former crack-shot deputy, has now become an embittered man ruined by a bad woman who forced him to turn to the bottle and become the laughing stock of the town. But Chance needs him again, and Chance believes that Dude can once again become the great lawman he formerly was. Martin, like Brennan, has never been better, and even if he does succumb to song once during the movie, this is a dramatic performance of grit and compassion and his redemption becomes the focal point of the movie. As Dude goes cold turkey and his hands begin to shake uncontrollably, he thinks it best to quit his job as to not endanger Chance and the others. But this is only after the reluctant and shrewd Colorado agrees to come aboard.

Besides Chance's bonding with the boys (the tough love he administers to Dude and the kiss on the forehead of Stumpy), Chance becomes smitten by the quite lovely Feathers (Angie Dickinson), a woman with a past. Feathers appears first on a handbill circulated to sheriffs in the territory, warning them of her presence and potential to cheat at cards. When it appears she is gaming and doing just that, she embarrasses Chance by challenging him to search her for the missing aces from the deck. When it turns out that

Feathers is innocent, she and Chance start emitting sparks and passion erupts between them. But in the universe of John Wayne, that means his virtue always casts him as the gentleman. She even goes so far as to camp outside his room all night for his protection, and when she invites him to sleep in her room, in her bed, she adds that she will sleep in the comfy rocking chair. But even young boys know that she is literally throwing herself at the mature sheriff and he is doing his best to rebuke her efforts. Even when she appears later in the film wearing her former saloon singing costume, very revealing for the time, Chance lets her know that he wants her to wear that getup *only* for him, threatening to arrest her for indecency if she wears that costume in public. Of course she takes that slight (and rare) verbal exchange as "I love you" and she collapses into the Duke's arms, ready for him to take her away anywhere. Dickinson and Wayne form a marvelous passion-under-the-radar relationship, and Dickinson, always chatty and perky, holds her own with Wayne.

The film's only flaw is that the climax feels rushed. A hell-bent shoot-out follows the botched trade of Joe Burdette for Dude, with Stumpy flinging sticks of dynamite at the shack where the outlaws are holed up. This climactic action sequence is over before it begins. The conclusion seems abrupt, especially when our heroes are in danger. Throughout the entire movie, the heroes recover too quickly. When Chance is tripped up by a rope across the bottom of the staircase in the hotel and knocked out cold, and when the outlaws get the jump on bathing Dude, the audience senses our boys will be back in control much sooner than later. When these same outlaws make Chance, unarmed, go to the prison to bail out Joe, we know that the unseen Colorado will suddenly save the day. This flaw can be extended to the major villain, Nathan Burdette, who is a tad too upstanding and sensible to be the dastardly criminal he is projected to be. We all remember Scar from *The Searchers*. Who remembers John Russell as Burdette from *Rio Bravo*?

When it comes to a thrill ride and light-hearted romp, *Rio Bravo*'s the sort of Western that can be spelled "fun." The heroes are bold, even if emotionally scarred and physically flawed (in the case of Stumpy), but the virtuous outcome and happy ending is never in doubt. Only the unexpected ambush death of Chance's friend Wheeler (perennial Wayne cohort Ward Bond) early on shocks the audience (besides the cold-blooded slaughter of the innocent man in the saloon that causes Chance to arrest Joe). From this point on, the audience senses that the good guys will prevail, while the action and suspense will keep everyone entertained.

Ace in the Hole
Movie: 3.5; Disc: 4.0
Criterion

Billy Wilder's seldom-seen (until now) *Ace in the Hole* is a gem, a film noir variation that hits hard to the gut and lingers long after the end credits appear. Many critics claim that next to *Citizen Kane*, *Ace in the Hole* is the best newspaper expose put to film (although a few films give *Ace* a run for its money)!

Made in 1951, *Ace in the Hole* gains its strength primarily from two stellar starring performances and an ensemble cast of first-rate support. Kirk Douglas as ruthless reporter Chuck Tatum sizzles and, like an over-active volcano, erupts upon the screen with a performance that is among the actor's best. Jan Sterling plays the bleached blonde Lorraine (even Tatum criticizes her overdone hair coloring), the femme fatale, a performance with nuance that might well be the actress' best. The script co-written by Wilder allows each character to subtly reveal his/her inner truth.

Chuck Tatum is a former "ace" New York reporter now on the skids, bitterly resigned to work cheap for the Albuquerque, New Mexico newspaper until he regains his status by coming up with the story that will put him back on top. Brazenly Tatum enters the publisher's office, telling the owner Boot (Porter Hall) that he is worth $250 a week, but he will agree to work for only $50 (settling for $40 when Boot tells him the job is worth $60, demonstrating the good ethnics by which he runs his newspaper). It takes a year, but Tatum smells out the human interest story that will put him on top … when a collector of Mexican Indian mementoes gets himself half buried during a cave-in at the bottom of a sacred mountain tunnel of underground caverns. Even though he is fewer than 10 feet away from the rescuing arms of Tatum and others, the victim's two legs are buried and the fragile cave walls threaten to collapse. This situation does not allow an easy rescue. Taking his camera, Tatum interviews the man and gets his photo spread over page one. However, his human-interest story will only pay off if he can delay the man's rescue for one full week, in order to garner nationwide interest and coverage. The local engineer, owing his job to the local sheriff (Ray Teal) who is running for re-election, wants to booster up the ceiling and walls and get the trapped man Leo Minosa (Richard Benedict) out within 14 hours. But Tatum thinks of his own future first by telling the sheriff (whom Tatum promises to paint as a hero in his series of articles) to order the engineers to drill down from the top of the mountain, a rescue operation that will take the needed week. Soon Tatum and his young assistant Herbie Cook (Bob Arthur), a reporter who serves as Tatum's conscience, quit their jobs at the local dusty-town newspaper to sell their story to a big New York City newspaper for much more money and publicity.

Meanwhile, Minosa's much younger and sleazy wife Lorraine is ready to jump on the first bus out of town, having tried to leave the burly and unrefined Leo more than once. Always dressed in revealing dresses that show off her shape and speaking in film noir platitudes (she states she never prays because kneeling bags her nylons), the woman hates her marriage, hates living in a dusty rural town and, most of all, hates Leo. However, for the human-interest story to work, Lorraine must remain the faithful, crying and dedicated wife. In one interesting sequence, as Lorraine awaits the local bus with a suitcase in her hand, Tatum tells her that by tonight their roadside diner

Chuck Tatum (Kirk Douglas) and Lorraine (Jan Sterling)

will be mobbed with the potential of making tons of money within the next week. The camera stands stationary as the huge bus pans in front of the camera, completely filling up the frame. The audience is not sure whether Lorraine will board the bus or not, but as the bus starts to move and pulls out of frame, we see Lorraine walking towards the diner. It's a very clever and well-photographed sequence. Later, as Leo catches pneumonia and is near death, he asks for a priest to deliver last rites and mentions a special present he hid to give Lorraine. Tatum, now starting to feel guilty for endangering the man's life, finds the present, nicely wrapped, and presents it to Lorraine. Inside she finds a skimpy fur and throws it on the ground, enraged that Leo would give her something that cheap. Tatum, outraged, places the fur around her shoulders and neck, and commences to choke the breath out of the emotionally cold wife, telling her to wear the fur. She, in turn, picks up a pair of scissors lying on the bed and stabs Tatum in the gut. The audience hardly sees any blood at first, but for the rest of the movie Tatum walks around wobbly using his jacket to hide the wound that becomes much more serious as time goes on. But such sequences demonstrate the shallowness of her character. And when Tatum speaks of making the big time again, Lorraine attempts to seduce the hulking reporter, even while her husband lies trapped and dying. However, Tatum has enough decency to slap the woman around, telling her that's how she needs to look, worried, and with tears dropping from her eyes. Physical abuse never felt so right.

Of course the mountain scene becomes a carnival with big top tents, rides, food stands and campers jamming the landscape, waiting to hear the fate of the trapped Leo. When interviewed by the media, such spectators even argue over who was on the scene first. As if that matters one bit. Of course when Leo eventually dies and Tatum tells the crowd the sad news, the disappointed people quickly jump back into their vehicles that zoom away as the tents are dismantled and the quiet peacefulness of the past returns, without missing a beat. Tatum crawls back (remember, he is wounded, bleeding and dying) to his old newspaper and offers the services of a $1,000 a day

reporter to Boot … for nothing. With that declaration, Tatum falls forward dead, the end credits appearing as swelling music punctuates the drama.

Frequently *Ace in the Hole* comes too close to becoming a preachy thesis movie that threatens to overstate its moral outrage, but the performances of Douglas, Sterling, Teal and others root the film in realistic humanity. The quiet intensity of the doomed Leo, soot and dust covers his face, making him at times resemble the Wolf Man, but he always maintains his dignity and humanity. In direct contrast we have his wife Lorraine, who represents the worst qualities of the human species. And coming in between these two extremes is the complex Tatum, an audacious reporter desperately trying to get back where he believes he belongs … the Big Apple and the best newspapers. His doctoring up the story of a simple man trapped in the collapsed cave demonstrates the man's newspaper savvy. However, when he opts to make the man stay buried for one week when a 14-hour rescue is possible, only then do we start to despise the motives of Tatum and turn against him. However, his relationship with Lorraine and outrage about the manner in which she disgraces her marriage demonstrates that Tatum does possess a moral compass. He allows his career to over-power his morality and makes some unethical decisions. However, with dignity and sacrifice, Tatum falls to the floor like a sack of potatoes at the film's end, paying the ultimate price for the circus atmosphere and the unnecessary death of poor Leo. At least Tatum brings the priest in time to deliver the last rites to Leo.

Ace in the Hole features the typically gorgeous Criterion pressing, and black-and-white cinematography never looked better. The presentation is a two-disc set, featuring a second disk of worthwhile supplemental material, including a wonderful documentary on director Billy Wilder. *Ace in the Hole* (also known as *The Big Carnival*) has been hidden in the vaults for too long, and with this Criterion presentation, it can once again be viewed as one of the defining movies of the 1950s, and one of the best. A blu-ray edition has just recently been released by Criterion, and looks even better.

Meet Him and Die
(aka Pronto ad uccidere)
Movie: 2.5; Disc: 3.0
Raro Video

During the 1970s, during the peak of the Italian horror cycle and the Spaghetti Western genre, another genre was running wild in Italian cinema, the Eurocrime movie (and what the natives referred to as "polizieschi") flourished. Taking its inspiration from the classic American gangster films (not only the classics from the 1930s and the 1940s, but the action-fueled brutal police thrillers from the 1960s and 1970s), the Italian Eurocrime adds locale color (by way of the beautiful European landscapes and ancient cities), violence and a liberal dose of nudity and sex. These movies, even in their English subtitled versions, always seem to go over the top with amplified fight sound effects similar to the kind that made the kung-fu genre so campy and fun (even the fights are staged stiffly with dramatic pauses before an elbow goes into the chest or a knee gets buried into an over-bloated stomach). Even if the choreography is unnatural and the stereotypes of the crime genre too pronounced, these Italian Eurocrime movies approach the great B-thrillers of the 1940s and 1950s in the manner by which they deliver the goods providing fast-paced popcorn entertainment in a little over 90-minutes. Movies such as these will never become classics, but they are enjoyable time-wasters with interesting plots and chiseled performances that fill a lazy afternoon.

Meet Him and Die (1976), starring Ray Lovelock (known to American audiences as the star of *Let Sleeping Corpses Lie* [1974], one of the better Italian zombie movies), casts the handsome blonde actor as Massimo Toriani, an undercover cop whose dangerous assignment is basically to destroy the expanding Italian drug cartel. To make syndicate contacts as an insider, he first must rob a jewelry store so he can get arrested and thrown in prison. Massimo's cellmate, Piero (Heinz Domez), is a gang member working under drug kingpin Giulianelli (Martin Balsam), also serving time in the same prison. So this simple association allows Massimo to become known to the drug lord.

Massimo is housed with a third nasty customer who only wants to break every one of his bones, but the other friendlier cellmate, Piero, benefits from working for Giulianelli, a prisoner who can afford to buy full prison luxury. Those who work for him get wine delivered regularly to their jail cells. After Massimo proves himself by beating the sadistic cellmate to a pulp, Giulianelli brings Massimo into his criminal organization and thinks of the young boy as a son. But this is exactly the plan concocted by Police Commissioner Sacchi (Riccardo Cucciolla) so that Massimo can learn the identities of the major players in the Italian drug syndicate.

In one of the films more improbable sequences, one night a prison guard who works for Giulianelli escorts Giulianelli, Piero and Massimo out of the prison compound (with no other prison guards visible). Actually he leads them to the front of the secure inmate area where one large metal lock on one door keeps inmates inside. Massimo just happens to have a knife in his pocket that he uses to unscrew several screws which allows the lock to be removed easily. Then, in one of the weirdest prison sets ever conceived for the movies, an under-lit dark alley winds around the rear of the facility where a car waits to pick up the escapees and then speeds away. First of all the prison set is low-rent all the way, with multi-leveled cells appearing only on one wall of the compound, with a very large (and empty) cement courtyard taking up the rest of the vast set. And what prison would have a dark alleyway in back, allowing easy escape by cover of the night?

The film is filled with stylized violence and plenty of car chases. Director Franco Prosperi fills the screen with shots of squids exploding when bullets penetrate the victim's chest, or sometimes a bullet pierces the front windshield of a car, with the driver's head whipped back, then the camera cuts to a close-up showing a bloody forehead. Cars flip over in slow motion and lie still, suddenly erupting in a fiery explosion. But the movie's best action sequence occurs when Massimo, having gained the trust of the highest-level drug lord, drives a 16-wheeler with a cargo of eggs (some of which have been filled with drugs) to its destination. Along the winding and deserted rural highways, Massimo comes upon a fallen motorcycle and its blonde-haired driver sprawled across the middle of the road. Of course when Massimo investigates, the injured blonde turns out to be a very conscious male with a gun, who is joined by three assistants. All four kick Massimo unconscious. But without missing a beat, Massimo revives and races across the field to arrive at a spot where he too easily topples and steals the motorcycle carrying two of the four thugs. The two men in the truck try to drive the motorcycling Massimo off the road, but he manages to jump on the side of the truck and climb a side ladder to the top. When one of the thugs inside climbs up the ladder to shoot him, Massimo gets the drop on him, which leaves only one man left in the truck's cabin. Whipping around the outside of the front of the truck, Massimo quickly grabs a gun he hid above the driver's seat and forces the driver to stop the truck. When the driver refuses to name the man who hired him to steal his cargo, Massimo shoots the driver dead and resumes his delivery of the eggs. The sequence, very nicely filmed, features effective stunt work, becoming suspenseful and resulting in delivering the major action sequence of the movie.

Tension builds when Massimo, working with Piero, passes a young policeman who recognizes the undercover cop and calls out his name. Massimo, thinking fast to protect both of them, knocks the young cop unconscious and resumes his mission. Later while driving with Massimo, Piero spots a car trailing them and purposely drives to a rural dead-end. When Piero is about to shoot the young policeman inside, the cop yells out Massimo's last name and Piero shoots the cop dead. Quickly realizing that the young cop knew Massimo, Piero turns quickly with his gun pointed, but Massimo is already one step ahead and fires two rounds into his chest, killing Piero. Tension created when the undercover cop is about to be exposed is used for maximum effect.

An aging Elke Sommer has a supporting role as the "secretary" to Giulianelli, the crime lord, but she has wild desire for Massimo and they have a fairly ridiculous lovemaking scene, with Sommer almost posing for the camera. While Sommer is nude, she actually shows very little skin. When the camera shoots her in close-up, the screen blurs to offset her years. She still remains an attractive, mature woman.

When the police surround Giulianelli's boat to arrest him at the end, it seems all the eggs in his possession are drug-free, so he laughs in their faces knowing the most severe charge against him cannot be proven. But Massimo senses what is going on, as he races to the drug lord's house and finds all his syndicate partners shot dead. But when he hears a car start outside around the side of the house, Massimo races outside with his gun pointed and he has Elke Sommer in his sight, and upon that freeze frame the movie ends. Actually, the ending is quite intelligent, as it shows us what Sommer did as far as killing off the cartel and stealing the drugs (broken egg shells are briefly shown on a table near the massacre), but all is revealed without using any narration. Like most good movies, the narrative is told visually where the viewer has to connect the dots.

The only grating aspect of the movie is a rather annoying American country-pop-rock song that is used for the opening credits, the ending credits and snippets used throughout the movie. For an Italian Eurocrime movie, the song sounds like it belongs in some sort of *Smokey and the Bandit* movie, with its acoustic guitars, harmonica and flute. But the action sequences make us forget such out-of-place music.

Raro Video does a nice job working with a pristine 35mm print, with the color rich and vibrant. The package includes a nicely illustrated 12-page book with liner notes by Eurocrime historian Mike Malloy, whose on screen introduction to the movie is a hoot. Malloy is working on a feature-length documentary of the Eurocrime genre and he really knows his stuff. The print features the Italian soundtrack with English subtitles. The Blu-ray quality is very nice.

Gang War in Milan
Movie: 3.0; Disc 3:5
Raro Video

Italians are the masters of absorbing the pop icons of other cultures and re-visioning them. Italian Westerns, while never sharing the same terrain as John Ford or Howard Hawks, managed to play upon all the American Western stereotypes (think of the beginning of *Once Upon a Time in the West* with all those iconic Western faces in close-up), amp up both the visuals and the dramatic (think of evil Western villains in Italian movies such as the dastardly Henry Fonda or tainted heroes such as Clint Eastwood) to produce a new dimension of violence. The Italian horror film is mostly the same, with the sex and gore quotient accentuated and the intensity often operatic in execution. It is almost as if the Italians throw all the iconic components into a blender and turn the machine up to 10, to supercharge everything.

The Italian Eurocrime genre follows this pattern. *Gang War in Milan* (1973) offers recognizable tropes, mostly borrowed from American crime movies. Director Umberto Lenzi (who directed *Nightmare City* and *Cannibal Ferox*) seems to be having lots of fun translating the American crime movie to Italian standards. We have Toto Cangemi (Antonio Sabato), an unskilled and poor peasant from Sicily, who ventures to the big city of Milan with equally down and out pal Lino (Antonio Casagrande). Toto soon rises to become kingpin pimp of all the prostitutes in Milan, using an import produce market as his legal front.

Yet we still have those sugary sequences where Toto visits his lonely and aged mother in an expensive nursing home, pining to return to her native village before she dies. Then we have slick Roger Daverty (Philippe Leroy) as the rival French boss who controls the illegal drug trade and is attempting to muscle his way into Toto's business. Finally we have the third party, deported Sicilian Billy Barone (Alessandro Sperli), hired by Toto to get rid of Roger or make him an offer he cannot refuse (Barone is godfather to Lino and his performance takes on Brando-like proportions), to join in as a 50/50 partner (Roger wants to be the main boss and take a 70% controlling interest

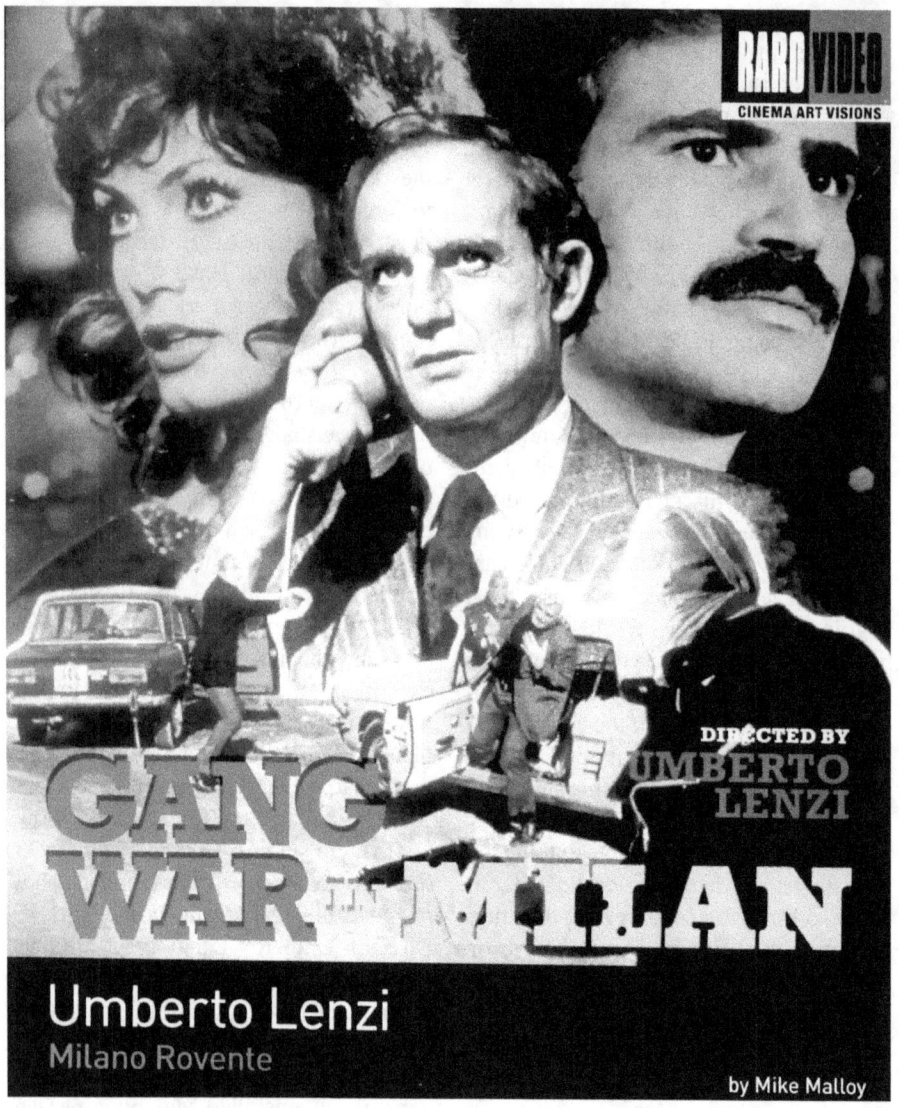

Umberto Lenzi
Milano Rovente

by Mike Malloy

in all operations). When Toto demands a fair 50% split, gang war breaks out in Milan and the bulk of the movie involves, as Laurel and Hardy made famous, a "tit for tat" series of violent retaliations with one gang attacking the other and retribution following. Into this mix come the women. We have Virginia (Carla Romanelli), who is the sweet innocent beauty (and mother) who wants to become a whore to earn a little extra cash. And there is the mysterious Jasmina (Marisa Mell), who is currently the girlfriend of one of the syndicate bosses in the French drug gang who immediately (too suddenly for comfort?) falls for and hops into Toto's bed.

Much of the movie involves gang bosses wining and dining one another or meeting in small crime-controlled nightclubs (wonderfully photographed with gaudy Technicolor hues), threatening what will happen if the one gang does not acquiesce to the demands of the other. However, the kid gloves come off pretty quickly as Roger's gang, posing as policemen, round up all of Toto's hookers and hold them for ransom. After making peace, all hell again breaks out with one speeding car carrying members of one gang surprising and attacking another car filled with members of the rival gang. Soon Roger's gang attacks Toto's prostitutes with knives and acid, blood streaming from their chests and throats. Even Toto, walking the Milan streets alone at night, is attacked by a carload of four thugs armed with push button switchblades (everyone in this movie loves to pause to listen to the sound of the switchblade open) who attempt to cut Toto to ribbons. But Toto's masterful fighting prowess armed with the sudden arrival of the police saves his ass.

Pretty soon the hired godfather's expertise with playing rough leads to Roger finally having to capitulate to Toto's demands and accept a partnership on Toto's terms. While Toto wanted to remain independent, the more conniving and ambitious Barone convinces Toto that the future of organized crime is not only women, but women and drugs. It becomes pretty apparent that Billy Barone is too greedy for his own good, and instead of Toto keeping a watchful eye on this well-schooled criminal veteran, he trusts the man because of his connection to his best friend Lino. But like a Shakespearean play, Toto has a tragic flaw, a self-serving lust for personal comfort involving wining and dining his mistress Jasmina and buying expensive resort villas, at the expense of paying money owed to Roger and his gang. In other words the business has finally been worked out for the good of both gangs, but Toto always makes Roger wait too long for overdue money owed. Finally, the experience and savvy of both Roger and Barone is no match for the naïveté of the too self-centered Tota. As we suspect, Roger has been paying Jasmina to bed Toto, become a trusted lover and get her hands on his cash. Near the film's end, she leaves the expensive villa with just that, hops a plane and delivers the money to Roger, for which Jasmina receives a nice check. At the same time Roger sets up Toto, framing him by stashing bags of pure heroin in a paper box placed atop his kitchen trashcan, just as the police arrive with a warrant to search the house. And by the movie's end Toto, on the run, finds Roger dead, a victim of Barone's plotting, as the godfather enters with Toto's gang announcing he has taken over all operations, approved by the gang. Of course in the final moments, Toto eyeballs his lifelong friend Lino (who endured a spectacular sequence of genital torture involving live electrical wires and a sizzling battery) standing side-by-side with his godfather Barone, and before Toto receives the Bonnie and Clyde Tommy-gun barrage fitting for a tragic hero, he fires a few shots into Lino, stating we started together and now we will end together. The film ends, quite appropriately, with Barone looking out at the Milan cityscape and calling it little Chicago.

To be quite honest, *Gang War in Milan* has it all. It has well-drawn characters, often little more than stereotypes, becoming strikingly larger than life personalities. The sets are nicely conceived and photographed and the story moves along at a brisk pace. The movie is nicely divided into thirds, with the first section detailing the invasion of Toto's gang by the Frenchman, the second section dealing with the gang war and retaliations and the final third dealing with the supposed peace between the gangs that only reveals the treachery instigated by Frenchman Roger and godfather Billy Barone. The movie is entertaining from start to finish and the Techniscope and Technicolor photography only adds to the thrilling visuals.

Raro Video worked with a pristine 35mm print and the Blu-ray digital transfer is outstanding, doing a good job of duplicating feel of Technicolor. Perhaps the DNR went a tad too far by eliminating grain and a true 35mm movie look, but the transfer is still outstanding in my opinion. The package arrives with an insightful, full-color 12-page booklet written by Eurocrime expert Mike Malloy, whose on screen video introduction is a true delight, as he is a real character. But his introduction is simply wonderful, filled with both personality and knowledge. The movie can be viewed in an English dubbed version or with the Italian soundtrack with English subtitles. For anyone who never got into the Italian crime genre, this is a good place to start.

The Gunfighter
Movie: 3.5; Disc: 3.5
Fox

Fox Home Video recently released a box set of three classic Westerns, none of which I ever saw before. Simply because of the exploitative title, I watched Henry King's *The Gunfighter* first, a movie starring Gregory Peck as the 35-year-old maturing gunslinger Jimmy Ringo, perhaps the fastest gun in the West. Featuring subtle, nuanced photography by Arthur Miller (a wonderful documentary on Miller appears on the disc as an extra), the movie is cited as one of the first adult Westerns, and this was in 1950, a full two years before *High Noon*.

What a revelation! *The Gunfighter* is a jaw-dropper and one of my favorite Westerns. The movie focuses upon claustrophobic set pieces (mostly saloons and small rooms) but becomes intensely visual by nature of Miller's cinematogra-

Marshal Mark Street (Millard Mitchell), Ringo's wife (Helen Westcott) and Ringo (Gregory Peck)

phy. The camera lingers on the grizzled faces (with Peck's Ringo sporting a big brimmed hat and bushy mustache, adding a world weariness to his tired eyes and haggard expression) and actors delivering well-honed dialogue. For a Western, the action is minimal and the dialogue expansive … but a more exciting Western film would be hard to find.

Seldom has a film captured the fatalistic, tough life of the reformed gunslinger, the man who is the target of every punk in every territory. Lawful towns do not want Ringo to remain, because his very presence threatens peace and quiet. Like today's media celebrity, Ringo is known everywhere and kids cut their classes and grown adults stop their workday to catch a glimpse of the demonic superstar.

Ringo, abandoned by a beautiful wife (Helen Westcott) and young son, returns to the town where they settled (she became the school teacher) to try to see both her and his son and convince them that he has changed, that their family has a chance to survive. He proposes moving to a distant territory where he is not known and buying a ranch, settling down and quietly living out the rest of their days. She is not totally convinced that such a dream could ever become reality, but her love for Ringo is genuine and, as he kisses his wife good-bye promising to return in one year for her answer, he heads out toward his horse and apparent assassination at the hands of three brothers avenging the death of their youngest brother (an energetic Richard Jaeckel). While the deputy catches two gang members perched inside a barn taking aim at Ringo, the third brother hides on the streets ready to take deadly aim.

Perhaps the most essential character is supporting character Marshal Mark Strett, played by chiseled character actor Millard Mitchell, perhaps his finest performance ever. Strett was a member of the same outlaw gang with Ringo, but Strett always kept a low profile. Citing an incident where an innocent girl was killed (any and all of the outlaws might have been responsible), the gang scattered and Strett ran to Cayenne and became a lawman, ironically re-inventing himself, but he reformed and became a damn fine man. Strett turned his entire life around and ruled the town with respect, opting not to carry a gun. Ringo, the handsome personality, could not abandon his former life so easily, but Strett does his best to protect his old friend and help him unite with his wife and son.

The moral ambiguity of the Old West has never been clearer with former outlaws wild in their youth suddenly reaching their middle years and looking at life differently, deciding they want to become family men and law-abiding citizens. However, their past won't let go. Strett is the rare exception of the man that Ringo emulates, and Ringo goes out of his way to tell his son that men like Strett should be his role model of what a great man can be. He admires his outlaw friend who escaped his past and craved a rich life of which he could be proud.

Gregory Peck, considered by many to be the last classic movie star of his era, proves his acting mettle with performances such as Jimmy Ringo in *The Gunfighter* (although, let's face it, his Atticus Finch from *To Kill A Mockingbird* will always be seen as his finest performance, as it should be). The sadness in Ringo's eyes, his understanding and hatred of having to kill young punks in order to stay alive and his dream to escape his past for a far more meaningful life just out of his grasp makes this performance one of Peck's best. Shockingly, *The Gunfighter* is a movie that slipped by me, and for anyone else in the same category, now is the time to watch this gripping Western drama, truly a classic of the 1950s.

**Warner Bros.
Gangsters Collection Volume 3**
Movies: *Mayor of Hell* (3.5);
Smart Money (3.0);
Picture Snapper (2.5);
Lady Killer (3.0);
Brother Orchid (3.0)
Warner Bros.

Warner Bros., deciding to combine their *Gangster* and *Tough Guys* DVD collections, has released the third *Gangster* collection, and it's a dandy. Unlike the horror film genre, gangster movies are generally divided into two categories: classics and the forgotten. The horror genre has fans of Poverty Row Monogram and PCR, and during the 1950s and beyond, B-directors are revered and studied as intently as the A list masters and classics. The same is true of film noir with a PRC production such as *Decoy* being held in high regard, along with classics such as *The Big Sleep, Out of the Past, The Postman Always Rings Twice* and *The Third Man*. When it comes to Warner Bros. and crime, the classics such as *Little Caesar,*

Ratsy Gargan (James Cagney) and his sweetheart Dorothy (Madge Evans)

Scarface and *Angles with Dirty Faces* are critiqued and praised. Edward G. Robinson, James Cagney and Humphrey Bogart are singled out for their work in the gangster genre, but most of the movies in this collection star one or more of the classic trio in lesser-mentioned, lesser-remembered and lesser-critiqued B-productions.

Let's start with *Mayor of Hell*, an important James Cagney entry that helped to start the subgenre (ignited in a few years by the Dead End Kids) of juvenile delinquency and troubled youth turning to organized crime to make their American dream come true. Frankie Darro plays Jimmy, the leader of a low-rent neighborhood gang of toughs. They start out offering to watch the cars of the well dressed for 25 cents, clearly marking the tires of all the patrons who pay. Ones who do not pay find their cars with flat tires, hood ornaments missing and broken windows. When these kids go too far by robbing and punching the owner of a candy store, who falls and cuts his head on broken glass, the gang is assigned to reform school. As each child and a parent appear before the sympathetic judge, the audience sees the reason why these kids are troubled youth. One parent, drunk, falls asleep in court. Other parents seem anxious to find their freedom by having their kids assigned to the reform school, thus taking responsibility away from them. A few parents are supportive and understand the second chance their child will gain from such rehabilitation, but the reform school is total Hell. Ruled by the lethargic and cruel taskmaster Mr. Thompson (Dudley Digges), the boys are fed unappetizing food, threatened with the whip, thrown into a solitary wooden cell that is too cold, etc. In such an environment, the boys are headed into a hard life of crime without any chance of reform.

James Cagney as Ratsy Gargan, the new Duty Commissioner, arrives feeling insulted that the local politicos passed him over for a cushy job he really wanted and instead gave him the reform school to oversee. He is what we would call a political ward leader, leader of a legal gang that supports one of the higher elected people in office and works hard to keep him in office. As a reward, such people are given political appointments. In a sense these legal political organizations are juxtaposed to the typical Warner Bros. syndicate crime ones, making the viewer consider … what makes a criminal gang criminal? Before long Gargan forces Thompson to take a month vacation leave while he, working with sweetheart and nurse Dorothy (Madge Evans), reorganize the entire operation of the reform school. Kids are elected to become mayor, police chief, treasurer (this pre-

Code movie makes the stereotyped Jew the treasurer), and there's a court where student lawyers try the cases. Of course one of the first cases involves one of the unruly delinquents who steals a candy bar from the school store, similar to the actual candy store robbery that landed these kids at reform school. But during the trial these same kids argue for justice and fairness and agree that one candy bar a day is enough. No one needs two.

Before long Gargan's own political gang is rebelling as his right hand man tries to wrestle the gang away from him. Gargan confronts the man, who draws a pistol. In a struggle the gun discharges and the gang member is severely wounded and Gargan runs and goes undercover, thus preventing him from returning to the reform school. Once Thompson returns and learns the truth, he again takes control of the school, returning its operation to the cruel former ways. However, this time the children rebel, charge the adults and force Thompson to climb a barn where, in a sequence similar to James Whale's climax from *Frankenstein*, he falls off the roof and lands on a barbed wire fence, dying a painful and bloody death, as the boys pick up torches and set the barn ablaze.

Frankie Darro, appearing as a pint-size version of Cagney, does a fantastic job teetering between hard-nose punk and a hopeful believer in the new ways initiated by Gargan. It's a multi-leveled performance. James Cagney, in his most dapper and energetic mode, creates a hip portrayal of a minor league politico who truly finds his calling and passion in life. In his ending monologue, he spits out the words and syllables so fast that audiences are amazed that he could speak that fast and form his thoughts so coherently. Contrasted to Darro, Gargan evolved from being a youngster who wanted his big payoff, to a man who truly cares about these young boys and wants to make the reform school a place where badasses can go straight. As directed by Archie Mayo, the film, re-filmed several times, is a wonderful crime drama with stellar acting and characterizations. Even the chief prison guard has a sympathetic sequence involving a sick inmate who is thrown into solitary to die. Fast paced and edited quite effectively, *Mayor of Hell* is a forgotten delight worth rediscovering.

The 1931 *Smart Money*, directed by Alfred E. Green, is surprisingly sophisticated for being an early talkie. The pristine print shimmers and the sound is full-bodied and not reedy or echoic. While not as dramatically satisfying as *Mayor of Hell*, *Smart Money* does an about-face with the screen persona of Edward G. Robinson, who recently completed his first classic movie, *Little Caesar*. In the earlier film he portrayed an Italian crime boss, loosely tailored after Al Capone, and in that film Robinson was hard-boiled, tough as nails and rather cruel. Most likely trying to avoid stereotyping, here Robinson plays Nick the Barber, a Greek from small town Irontown, U.S.A. In his barber shop Nick holds games of chance, mostly dice, where he is known as being lucky. He dreams aloud, among his close friends, that if he were ever staked with $10,000 he would win big for everyone and open a successful casino in the Big City. Without flinching, his pals chip in with the dough, and Nick, an honest man, promises to pay them back and split the profits with all of them 50/50. Suddenly, as the title card states, we find ourselves in "The City" as Nick searches out big-time gambler Hickory Short, the man he plans to slaughter for big stakes at poker. Prowling around the hotel where Hickory holds his poker games all night, Nick meets a blonde girl, Marie (Noel Francis), who works the gift/candy counter, and we learn that Nick has a weakness for blondes. She tells him where to find the room where the poker game is held. Unfortunately, another big time operator, Sleepy Sam (Ralf Harolde), pretends to be Hickory Short, but Sam is corrupt and works in cahoots with the other players to flimflam suckers. Before long the $10,000 is gone and Nick is given the bum's rush.

As the movie progresses, Nick gets wise, builds up his bankroll and plays Sleepy Sam one on one, having his boys (one of whom is played by James Cagney, the only time these two stars appeared together in the same film) back him up with pistols just outside the hotel door. Nick

knows when he wins big, Sleepy Sam's gang will get rough and not allow him to waltz out the door with their money. But Nick wins big and survives to reap the benefits.

Soon Nick sets up a barbershop in the Big City and his name is not connected with the gambling establishment he owns, but the D.A. is out to nail the smooth operator, and Nick's weakness for all things blonde and female leads to his downfall. Along the way this pre-code film eludes sexual innuendo and racist dialogue that was natural for the time. Edward G. Robinson as Nick the Barber, while cocky, wins audience sympathy because of his personal morality. He accepts money from his friends, but he will die before betraying them. As money comes his way and fame follows, Nick's weakness for the ladies ultimately makes him humble. After shooting a person, he is sent up the river for 10 years (he brags he might get lucky and get out in five), as his black friend offers him a rabbit's foot for luck, something he did earlier in the film. Nick smiles and states the rabbit foot never brought him luck, so instead he rubs his friend's head for luck, laughing at his fate, playing out the cards life dealt him. Nick is never less than likable, and his sense of humor maintains his humanity. Also as his arrogance melts by self-awareness and humility, he learns the error of his ways and understands his penalty is just. As his media star rises, he is always dressed to the nines but handcuffed to a policeman as reporters ask to take his photo, which he gladly does but always covering the handcuffs with his coat to preserve his dignity. Nick the Barber is a truly interesting character, one that audiences would enjoy being around. And for 1931 Edward G. Robinson, this little forgotten crime drama only testifies that Robinson was an actor of mushrooming talent at the beginning of a wonderful film career.

Picture Snatcher, made in 1933 and directed by Lloyd Bacon, shows the transformation of James Cagney from 1931 to 1933. Not yet an established star when he co-starred in *Smart Money*, James Cagney was handsome yet bland in the earlier production. But by 1933 Cagney settled comfortably into his screen persona of gentleman gangster, a fast-talker with big dreams. The movie begins as Cagney leaves prison after being shot six times, vowing to go straight because the criminal life did him wrong. The old gang celebrates his release, and even though he is given his share of the robbery money with interest, he is not interested. "I quit," he smirks, and he means it too. His contact Al McLean, a newspaperman he met in prison, offers him a job, but when Cagney comes into the newspaper office, Al tells him there's no money in this racket. The newspaper he works for is virtually a tabloid, a rag, with little prestige and even less money. But an opportunity arises for Danny (Cagney) to become a picture snatcher, a photographer, and his first gig is to get a picture of a fireman who was called to the scene of his own house burning down, with his dead wife in bed ... along with her lover. Hennessy the fireman (Pat Collins) is depressed and suicidal. He sits alone in the burned out ruins of his house, armed with a firearm, threatening to shoot anyone who attempts to exploit his misery. Clever Danny pretends to be the insurance adjuster who is doing an inventory on the damage, but when he eyes a photo of the fireman and his wife framed on the wall, he sneaks the photo into his jacket and flees. The photo becomes front page news, but Hennessy comes storming into the newspaper office, threatening to kill Danny, and thus a hard-hitting drama escapes into glorious moments of comic insanity as Danny creeps and crawls beneath desks, trying to escape, finally sneaking into the ladies bathroom where he meets the equally fast-talking Allison (Alice White), a hard-as-nails sexpot who falls for the handsome photographer. Later Danny meets and falls in love with the well-bred Pat (Patricia Ellis), the daughter of the cop who sent Danny up the river, and after they break up and get back together, Al takes Pat to meet Danny, who just happens to be in his car being seduced by Allison. Using his best comedic timing, Danny has to knock the blonde unconscious and toss her into the back seat so Pat cannot see that he was with another woman. The tone of the movie constantly vacillates from drama to comedy, and the expertise of Cagney manages to turn all these tone changes around perfectly. In one very unsettling scene, Danny's old criminal friend Jerry the Mug (Ralf Harolde who played an equally sleazy character from *Smart Money*) is holed up in his apartment shooting it out with the cops, when Danny appears. Forcing the criminal to be off guard, Jerry turns around allowing the police to machine gun him to ribbons, while Danny snaps the photo of the man in his death throes. However, he gives Pat's father credit for bringing the man in and Dad once again gets his stripes back.

Picture Snatcher is not a great film by any means, it is decidedly mediocre, but the always changing tone of the film with the emerging star turn by James Cagney makes this seldom seen crime movie memorable. The film shifts easily from hardcore violence to comedic and romantic shenanigans effortlessly. And for 1933, this was very strong stuff, delivered with a one-two combination punch.

Lady Killer, another 1933 production, demonstrates the star persona that James Cagney brought to the gangster genre. This Roy Del Ruth directed crime/comedy is delightful for its hard-as-nails dialogue and its changing tone and mood shifts. The persona crafted by Cagney here is so well defined and confident that everyone knew this was a star in the making.

The movie starts off as Dan Quigley (James Cagney), a movie theater usher, is warned not to be late for work, but late he is, his dirty hands fingering dice. When a prissy older woman with her dog tries to enter the theater, Dan is polite yet firm that rules are rules, the dog is not allowed. The lady complains to management. Dan's boss enters the scene, reminding Dan that this is the latest complaint of many that patrons made against him, so he is fired. Without missing a beat Dan sees the beautiful Myra Gale (Mae Clarke) drop her purse as she enters a cab. Demonstrating that he is an upright type of guy, Dan tracks the woman down to return her purse. Just by chance, her brother-in-law informs Dan that a "friendly" poker game is being waged in the side room, and Dan invites himself to play. Douglas Dumbrille as Spade runs the operation, and Dan loses his money, keeps his sense of humor and leaves. He soon finds out that Myra is a con woman who drops her purse at the flick of an eyelash, to lure suckers into the crooked poker game. When Dan discovers the truth, he huffs and puffs and forces himself back into Myra's apartment and confronts the chiselers, forcing them to give his money back and then he demands they make him part of the team. Dan personally guarantees that his more creative cons will make the gang even more money. His one rule is that no one gets hurt; no muscle or violence can ever be used. Of course one of the poker/gangster gang kills one of the victims and the police are immediately all over the gang. Dan quits the gang and, without a dime, heads West where he breaks into the movies, doing bit parts (including being spray-painted to play an Indian, with headdress and all) until star Lois Underwood (Margaret Lindsay) notes Dan's potential and gets him set up for the starring roles. Of course money and stardom results, as does his distinguished mustache that he now sports to proclaim his leading man persona. It is not long before the gang catches up with Dan and threatens to expose his past, unless blackmail money is paid. For $10,000 the gang promises to leave town, but pretty soon the gang is stealing money from the wealthy at ritzy Hollywood parties. Even though things get crazy during the final reel, the movie ends satisfactorily with Dan clearing his name, marrying Lois and resuming his role as Hollywood star.

Dan (James Cagney) now sports the movie star mustache and poses with Lois Underwood (Margaret Lindsay).

The cleverness of the script involves Dan getting bigger and better Hollywood roles because the studio heads note the sudden increase in fan mail that young girls are writing him. Based upon such fan mail, the studio heads decide to feature Dan in more prominent roles. However, in the next sequence we see the conniving Dan write page after page of fan mail, realizing that such an endeavor will pay off big time for him. Later, once he is a star, now eating in the finest restaurants, wearing the most fashionable tailored clothes, Dan becomes upset by a review a famous critic writes about Lois and him. It just so happens this same critic is eating across the table from Dan, and in his warm manner Dan invites the critic to talk inside the men's room. While the critic repeats over and over that he is entitled to his opinion, Dan tells him to write about the movies and not about the personal lives of the stars involved. To drive his point home, he forces the critic to eat his own column. Before pushing the arrogant man into an open bathroom stall, he threatens to cut off his ears and mail them to his folks. Later, even after the gang refuses to leave Hollywood, even having the audacity to rob precious jewels from Lois' home, Dan intercepts the gang, roughs them up a tad and demands to have the jewels so he can return them. In such sequences Dan's buster and energy, presented as a likable rogue manner, demonstrate his code of honor and his expectation for people to keep their word. When people lie to Dan or try to cheat him, the hardcore criminal emerges from the debonair Hollywood persona and all Hell breaks loose. Cagney delivers a star turn and his performance, equal parts gangster and Hollywood movie star, crackles, snaps and pops. The screenplay by Ben Markson and Lilie Hayward sizzles and allows Cagney the latitude to shine and dominate the screen. *Lady Killer* is seldom seen yet features a wonderful James Cagney, and the film

deserves to be re-evaluated, simply for being a different take on the traditional gangster movie.

By 1940 Edward G. Robinson's gangster persona was so well defined that *Brother Orchid*, directed by Lloyd Bacon, was a long overdue spoof of the genre. Robinson plays "Little John" Sarto, the leader of a big city crime syndicate. At the peak of his power, feeling unsatisfied, Johnny gives up his leadership of the gang to the ambitious Jack Buck (Humphrey Bogart, one year before his international fame in *The Maltese Falcon*). Sarto wants to travel to Europe and experience the *good life* that has always been elusive to him. However, while traveling aboard, he finds the same con artists, grifters and criminal types that he encountered in his own backyard. Coming back home five years later, Sarto wants to step back into his gangland leadership, but Buck will have none of that. In fact Buck would rather kill Sarto than give up his authority and newfound power.

Meanwhile Robinson renews his half-hearted relationship with Flo (Ann Sothern), a blonde floozy with a big heart who would do anything to make Little John happy. However, Robinson is big on the promises but slow to deliver the ring and take the marriage vows. Setting up a meeting with Johnny and Buck at a little supper club to make peace, Flo learns too late that she has in fact set up her boyfriend for the long, final ride. When Buck's gang is driving him to the woods for the kill, the last image Sarto has of Flo is one of her waving and smiling, Little John thinking his girl is happy to see him "get it!" However, once Buck turns up the car radio and the two hired guns escort Sarto deeper into the woods, Sarto snaps a branch hitting their heads and the little guy makes a run for freedom, collecting a bullet or two before falling near the water's edge. The hit men assume the deed is done, but Sarto, still alive, crawls to a monastery and there is rescued and nursed back to health.

The monks at the monastery raise flowers, which they sell in the city, giving all the profits to the poor. Sarto, who is impressed by a life of self-sacrifice and doing the right thing for others (an alien concept in his world, to say the least), willingly wants to join the monk's order, re-naming himself Brother Orchid. Impressed with sandals (he calls them air-conditioned shoes) and non-fashionable clothing (he balks at having his head shaved, claiming he has to think about his looks), Brother Orchid adjusts to his new life of hard work. Still, the old con artist rears up inside and Orchid gets into trouble when he promises to pay a young boy to do some of his assigned labor while he naps on a blanket under a table. Orchid has no money and is conning the boy, but soon Brother Superior (Donald Crisp) slyly admits that he pulled some of the same stunts when he first entered the order. One day a dejected Brother Superior tells Orchid that the order is no longer allowed to sell flowers in the city because they doesn't pay protection money, and the wizened former criminal figures out quickly that Jack Buck's syndicate is behind the squeeze. Orchid reads that his former girl Flo is about to marry a rich Texas rancher Fletcher (Ralph Bellamy), so he leaves the monastery to put his affairs in order. Quickly discovering that Fletcher really loves Flo (he loves her too, but his new life of self-sacrifice allows him to step aside for the better man), Orchid makes friends with Fletcher and his Texas buddies and uses them to invade Buck's highly fortified offices. There, with almost comical music accenting the lighter tone, Orchid and Buck have a fistfight that establishes Orchid as the better man. The police finally arrive and arrest the gang, once again allowing the monks to sell their flowers in town.

By the final minutes of the movie, Brother Orchid returns gleefully to the order stating this is the world where he found the class he was always seeking out, and with the problems of his former life resolved, Orchid can resume his life as Brother Orchid and live off the bounty of the land.

James Cagney played a bland supporting character to Edward G. Robinson in *Easy Money*, not having refined the vivacious screen persona he would be famous for creating. Humphrey Bogart plays a similar second banana stereotype, as the rival gang boss in *Brother Orchid*. But Bogart's performance, while effective, lacks the bombast that defined his later and classic screen persona. In these high-flying days, Robinson was top dog and, many of the stars whose careers would soon eclipse his, fine-tuned their acting chops by performing supporting roles in Robinson star vehicles.

Brother Orchid is not a great film by any means, but it is a damn fine Robinson performance in a movie that smiles at the formerly hardcore gangster movie genre. Robinson's "Little John" Sarto is marvelous, a man who has mastered his criminal life and risen to the top, only to feel empty and dissatisfied, looking for a way to fill the void in his life. Thinking a life of travel and high living is the answer, Sarto gives up his criminal crown, but after five years, he realizes he still feels unfulfilled. And little by little Sarto begins to understand that his perverse morality needs adjusting and that all he needs to do is embrace the simple life of a monk. *Brother Orchid* demonstrates it's never too late to change and turn one's life around, and that sometimes the life we have chosen for ourselves is not the one that best satisfies our needs.

The Warner Bros. box set is filled to the brim with impressive (and early) performances of stars associated with the Warner gangster genre. And even before they were stars, these lesser productions demonstrate the impressive work created by Robinson, Cagney and Bogart before they hit the big time. And each digital print looks gorgeous.

Marnie
Movie: 2.5; Disc: 3.0
Universal

By 1964 Alfred Hitchcock's career was beginning a gradual decline, but even when it comes to his less-than-stellar movies, the consummate cinematic style of Hitchcock continues to shine. After blonde sexpot Tippi Hedren made such an impact in 1963's *The Birds*, one year later Hitch wanted to feature his newfound star in a star-making performance. So the odd *Marnie* resulted, starring Hedren as a serial thief that robs more for her psychological need than for the money. Changing jobs, hair color and names as easily as she produces a wallet full of phony ID cards, Marie Edgar gets herself hired as secretary to Mark Rutland (Sean Connery in his best James Bond mode), a man who recognizes the woman as a criminal. Yet Rutland is both intrigued and attracted carnally to such damaged goods, and he wants to put her in the position where she might strike again. Of course during the first week in the office Marnie notices that the office manager cannot remember the combination to the big office safe, so he writes the number down on a piece of paper which he locks in the desk drawer not far from the safe. Marnie can easily get that key from another office secretary. So one night she hides in the bathroom stall allowing everyone to exit at the end of the workday, and she opens the desk drawer, gets the lock combo and opens

Mark Rutland (Sean Connery) and Marnie (Tippi Hedren) seem concerned.

the vault. Unknown to her, a custodian is washing the floors just down the hall from the small office in which the safe is located, and his wet mop slowly approaches. The way Hitchcock has cinematographer Robert Burks frame the shot, the audience able to see Marnie work the safe while the custodian approaches, creates maximum tension. Once Marnie empties the money into an envelope that dangles from her side pocket, she takes off her shoes to tiptoe past the custodian and exit down the side staircase. However, the envelope plops to the floor loudly as Marnie stops dead in her tracks, but luckily the worker does not hear a thing. Of course, Marnie changes her hair back to blonde and Rutland traces the now-fleeing criminal to a horse stable, where he confronts her. Rutland replaces the missing money himself and wants Marnie to come clean.

Long periods of psychobabble (think of the end of *Psycho*) waylay the production, and the audience is curious why sequences occur where Marnie visits her mother in Baltimore, sequences where her mother shows very little interest in her. Rutland concludes that something occurred during Marnie's childhood that resulted in her serial thievery and that the solution to her damaged psyche lies with her mother in Baltimore. Hitchcock's conclusion occurs back in Baltimore, where Marnie comes to learn her mother was a prostitute who awoke her in the middle of the night so she and her sailor client could use her bed, while she slept on the couch. One night a john gets a might too interested in the sleeping daughter, molesting the child before mother intervenes. The young Marnie kills the man, but the mother takes the blame. Only subconsciously remembering the horrible course of events, Marnie goes into fits whenever she sees the color red (the screen flashes red in the worst sense of a William Castle movie gimmick), reminding her subconsciously of the blood-splattered corpse. But once this confession occurs, and mother and daughter break down in tears, Marnie is miraculously cured and Rutland and she can pursue a normal married life together.

Of course while the plot sometimes gets ridiculous and overblown, and Tippi Hedren's underwhelming performance lets the production down at every opportunity, the Hitchcock style comes through and invigorates the movie. Besides the sequences already mentioned, we have a marvelous point-of-view sequence with Marnie riding her wild, out-of-control horse as she approaches a stone fence at a nearby home. The horse is not prepared to jump, so we see the horse breaking its leg and Marnie pleading with the woman in the house to give her a gun to put the horse out of its misery. Such

sequences are exciting and pure visual Hitchcock. While *Marnie* has many more flaws than the typical Hitchcock film, it is nonetheless a gripping suspense thriller with much merit.

The Baron of Arizona
Movie: 3.0; Disc: 3.5
Criterion Collection

Three years before achieving horror film stardom in *House of Wax*, Vincent Price made a quirky low-budget movie for director Samuel Fuller early on in the director's career. *The Baron of Arizona* was based upon an actual historic figure, the arrogant and crafty con artist James Addison Reavis, the self-proclaimed Baron of Arizona. While the movie is not a Western in the traditional sense, it is in fact an odd-duck movie that affords Vincent Price a tailor-made role becoming one of his finest performances. In an overly complex plot, Reavis finds an orphaned Mexican girl and creates a noble lineage for her, making her the only survivor of the Peralta family, a family that Reavis concocts that holds the land rights to the ownership of the state of Arizona. Of course none of this is true, and most of the movie's plot concerns Reavis' efforts to forge land grants and paperwork that put this elaborate hoax into reality. After all his ducks are in a row, Reavis marries the girl so he can become the Baron to her Baroness.

Vincent Price, never an actor of great subtlety, has some marvelous sequences. In the film's opening moments, entering the muddy adobe home during a very rare rain storm in the Southwest, Reavis takes off his dripping hat and loosens his coat, all smiles, realizing he has found the central character in his fantastic scheme ... the little Sofia. Later Reavis joins an order of monks, living a humble life of labor at the monastery, hoping to gain access to their library that houses land rights. Concocting his own chemicals and liquid, he can erase ink and redo writing with ink identical to the original print. He comes to find that another copy of the land grant is held by a Spanish noble, and for this Reavis has to become a Gypsy and live with a Gypsy band. The entire story stretches reality, but this larger-than-life con allows Vincent Price to create a masterful over-the-top performance that he does so well.

By the final third of the movie, Reavis squares off in federal court with his worthy adversary John Griff (Reed Hadley), the government prosecutor who is sworn to prove that the self-proclaimed Baron of Arizona and his wife are counterfeits and that their claim to owning the entire state and all its assets is unfounded. And Reavis relishes the courtroom battle.

The film gets bogged down in such heavy-handed plotting and the script is filled with dialogue and little action. Still, watching one of the screen's finest con artists do his thing is sometimes mesmerizing, and Price submits a masterful performance. The film's final minutes become suspenseful and animated when vigilante justice takes over and the local town mob rounds up Reavis to hang for his crimes. At first escaping with help from Sophia's guardian, Reavis is finally trapped in his own office, a large room framed by a giant map of Arizona behind his desk. Over the rafters a rope is slung and, in one of his best acting sequences ever, Price delivers an impassioned speech explaining why the locals can only win this case by keeping him alive. Seconds away from death, the wily and now terrified rodent speaks the truth and he even survives the noose that is tightening around his throat. Griff is able to prove that the ink used to forge the documents was not authentic, and Reavis admits to his crimes, serving several years in prison. However, after serving his prison time, exiting, he once again walks through the pouring rain as a carriage greets him, one filled with all his loved ones and friends, including wife Sofia, who stood by him and will continue to do so.

Shockingly, for a film released in 1950, this Criterion Collection print is merely okay, not pristine as we generally expect. The opening sequences are soft and sometimes flare from replacement footage or over-exposure. The print is never up to typical Criterion standards. However, for preserving this little seen Samuel Fuller film, which he both wrote and directed, this is as good as it will ever get. For all fans of Vincent Price, *The Baron of Arizona* is a must-see movie.

www.ingramcontent.com/pod-product-compliance
Lightning Source LLC
Chambersburg PA
CBHW081727100526
44591CB00016B/2533

9781936168460